Just Being:

A Pagan Guide to Meditation

by Shanddaramon

Just Being

Just Being:

A Pagan Guide to Meditation

by Shanddaramon

Just Being

Just Being
A Pagan Guide to Meditation
by Shanddaramon

First Edition (Softcover)
Published by:
Astor Press
http://www.astorpress.com

Copyright © 2009, Shanddaramon

ISBN: 978-0-578-02611-4

All rights reserved. No Part of this book may be reproduced or transmitted in any form or by any means, electronic or mechanical, including photocopying, recording or by any information storage and retrieval system, without written permission from the author, except for the inclusion of brief quotations with proper annotation.

Produced in the United States of America

The author may be contacted at mail@shanddaramon.com.
For more information visit http://www.shanddaramon.com.

Dedication

This book is dedicated to my long time friend and meditation partner Sydney. He was a cat who lived with me for 19 years. He would often sit next to me during my meditation sessions or jump in my lap while I wrote on the computer and would stay there for hours offering love, support, and guidance. I will miss him every time I sit down to meditate or write.

Just Being

Acknowledgments

The experiments and experiences that led to the writing of this book have come from years of studying and practicing meditation. They have also come from years of teaching meditation to a variety of students. I wish to take this opportunity to thank those students for their patience and for sharing their thoughts with me.

Table of Contents

Preface	11
Why I Wrote This Book	11
A Description of the Chapters	13
Developing Meditation Skills	14
How To Use This Book	16
When Things Are Not Going Well	18
Exercises	19
Chapter One	**21**
What is Meditation?	21
Introduction	21
Defining the Term	21
Why Meditate?	28
What Happens In Meditation?	30
Types of Meditation	39
Physical Meditations	40
Mental Meditations	42
Emotional Meditations	43
Spiritual Meditations	45
The Stages of Meditation	45
Summary	46
Exercises	46
Chapter Two	**51**
How To Meditate	51
(The Outer Procedure)	51
Introduction	51
Reasons for Disappointment	52
Preparing to Meditate – the Four Ps	57
Developing a Meditation Procedure	61
Summary	67
Exercises	67
Part One - Stretching	68
Part Two - Centering and Collecting	81
Part Three – Connecting and Disconnecting	83
Part Four – Entering In and Exiting	86
Part Five – Invocation and Release	88
Part Six – Intent and Acknowledgment	90

Table of Contents

    Part Seven – Putting It All Together..................92

Chapter Three..................97

  The Four Stages of Meditation..................97
  (The Inner Procedure)..................97
    Introduction..................97
    Relaxation..................98
    Concentration..................99
    Acceptance..................101
    Absorption..................103
    Combining the Stages..................106
    Summary..................106
    Exercises..................107
      Part One – Relaxation..................107
      Part Two – Concentration..................116
      Part Three – Acceptance..................130
      Part Four – Absorption..................146
      Part Five – Combined Procedure..................153

Chapter Four..................157

  Pagan Meditations..................157
    Introduction..................157
    Exercises..................158
      Part One – Physical Meditations..................158
      Part Two – Mental Meditations..................174
      Part Three – Emotional Meditations..................189
      Part Four – Spiritual Meditations..................198
      Part Five – Open Meditation..................207

Chapter Five..................211

  Beyond Meditation..................211
    Introduction..................211
      Part One – Meditation Tools..................212
      Part Two – Life As A Meditation..................214
    Exercises..................216

Appendices..................223

  A Group Pagan Cakes and Tea Ceremony..................223
  A Meditation Journal Format..................225
  A Meditation Practice Check-Off Sheet..................228
  Resources..................233

>   Source Books...233
>   Related Books..234
>   Web Pages...235
>   Indices...236
>   Exercises...236
>   Illustrations..239

Preface

Why I Wrote This Book

"I can't meditate." I've heard this phrase being spoken countless times by my students and by many others. The ongoing rush of daily life that calls out for our attention at every turn makes it difficult to slow down our thoughts and to quiet our minds. Yet, few would disagree that meditation is an important part of most any spiritual practice. This is especially true for those of us who call ourselves Neo-Pagans (or just Pagan with a capital P for short). Modern Paganism embraces mysticism and the beauty and wonder of Nature. Both of these things call us to meditate – to soften the critical mind in order to get in touch with the greater mystery of life and with Spirit. But, that fact often does not make it any easier to still a busy mind. It is for my students and all other Pagans who feel a calling to listen to Spirit, the mystery of Nature, and to their inner selves that I have written this book. This text will be a guide on how to meditate but, more than that, it will reflect upon the unique way in which meditation can strengthen and deepen the study and practice of Paganism.

I once taught a college course on meditation. I saw first hand how meditation can change people and their outlook on life. The course encouraged students to explore different meditation techniques from different religious perspectives and, in the process, provided ways for them to delve deeply into themselves. Through the study of many forms of contemplative spiritual practices, engaging in group meditation, and keeping a meditation journal, students often awakened a part of themselves rarely touched before in other studies. It was rewarding for me to see those young people, many of whom eschewed anything religious, find their individual spiritual nature through meditation. Having taught the class for several years, I was able to test out several different methods and ideas and, thereby, hone my teaching of the class. Much of what I learned from teaching that class has been put into this book.

Meditation has been an important part of my own practice as well. I first became interested in the subject as a child because of my asthma. As a young boy I became convinced that health was intimately related to the condition of the whole body and mind. Medication was able to help me when I had asthma attacks but it was less effective in preventing the attacks from happening in the first place. Asthma can be triggered by many things including allergic reactions, airborne irritants and particles, exercise, and extreme weather conditions, just to name a few of the many challenges. It can also be caused by emotional conditions such as fear and worry. In order to try and prevent those life-threatening asthma attacks from coming on, I needed to try and avoid both environmental and emotional triggers. The former threat involved physical remedies but the latter required mental control – control that I learned could be sought through the practice of meditation. It was through this practice that I was able to experience a state of peace and tranquility. My meditation practice gave me a place of emotional respite in my mind where I could go when the outside world seemed threatening. Later, I began to study Eastern religions, many of which make meditation a central part of spiritual development. It was then that I was able to begin to understand the relationship of meditation to a connection with the higher self and beyond. Those lessons stayed with me when I discovered modern Paganism.

In some religions, spiritual development is encouraged by the teachings of a mentor or church official. Students of Paganism can also learn by studying with a mentor but it is not necessary. Direct training and experience is often sought in Pagan spiritual development and meditation can be an important part of that experience. I started my Pagan studies with a High Priestess who taught me many things but I soon found out I needed to branch out on my own. A critical part of my personal development as a solitary practitioner came through my own meditations. I began to develop my own five degree system for learning and growing which became the focus of my first book *Self-Initiation for the Solitary Witch*. Most of the lessons for the higher degrees of that book include some type of meditation. I learned that studying with a teacher can be very helpful but I also learned to trust my own heart and body. When the meditation was going well, my body felt it. It just felt right.

Another reason I wanted to write this book was because there are many meditation books but none that I found that are focused on modern Pagan spiritual principles. Paganism is a growing spiritual tradition in the world and one that I believe can offer the world a truly religious alternative. If meditation is an important part of Pagan practice then there needs to be a meditation book that can address the specific spiritual needs of Pagans. You can read generalized books on meditation but there will come a time in your practice when you will want to connect your meditation practice to your own spiritual practice. I believe that spiritual meditation is about connecting to that place that is deep within us but which is the same as the mystery that is beyond us as well. If you find that place to be full of the gods or sacred cosmic energies or your higher self or whatever higher concept you may embrace, then you have found where Pagan spiritual principles and good meditation practice converge.

A Description of the Chapters

In the first chapter we will attempt to understand the general meaning of meditation. We will do this by exploring various definitions. Then, we will explore the reasons that people often begin a meditation practice and ask if those reasons are realistic by comparing them to the actual benefits of meditation. Next, we will go deeper by understanding how meditation relates to various states of mind and different meditation practices. Finally, I will share with you what I believe to be the four stages of meditative practice which will become a major focus of the remainder of the book.

Chapter Two begins our exploration of how one learns to meditate. You will learn how to prepare yourself to begin a meditation practice and then study specific procedures you can use to develop a successful practice. The development of these preliminary practices is what I call T*he Outer Procedure*. We will discuss those things which may cause your practice to be less effective including the variety of things that can distract your mind away from its goal. Part of every good developing meditation practice is learning to be able to review what has been done and how well it worked. You will learn how to do just such a review. This chapter will also include a great number of exercises that will help you develop specific skills you will need to begin and continue a deep and effective practice.

While Chapter Two focuses on developing an overall Pagan meditation procedure, Chapter Three looks at specific goals for meditation – the central focus of a meditation practice. This is where the truly challenging but ultimately meaningful work will begin. This chapter will explore my theory of the four stages of meditation: relaxation, concentration, acceptance, and absorption. Each stage will be examined separately in detail and exercises will be provided to develop your skills in each. The culmination of these practices will be to develop what I call T*he Inner Procedure*.

Chapter Four will provide some meditations specifically designed for Pagans. We will explore meditations that use Pagan spiritual principles to develop the self and one's connection to the universe and its many cycles.

The final chapter, Beyond Meditation, will explore things related to meditation such as keeping a meditation journal and items that can be purchased or made to help with your practice. This chapter will also discuss how meditation can become an important part of your everyday life and will include some final exercises.

In the Appendices you will find scripts that can be used to create your own meditation tapes.

Developing Meditation Skills

Meditation is both simple and complex. It is both easy and challenging. In essence, meditation is just sitting in a state of pure awareness but, for many people, just sitting for any great length of time is a great challenge. The image that most people have of meditation is that someone sits down in a full lotus position (both legs crossed with feet resting on each knee) and then begins to enter a deep meditative state. On the surface, it seems like that is all a meditator is doing but that is not always the case. Practicing meditation is a skill. In fact, it is a combination of many skills each of which needs to be learned, developed, and practiced. Like any complex activity, it helps to learn and master each specific skill separately and then combine those skills to create a complete and deep meaningful meditation practice. Please do not let the idea that you are developing a skill send you packing, however. Learning to meditate is a joyful and pleasurable experience and developing the skills to do it well does not have to be a difficult and unwieldy process.

Think back to when you first learned to drive a car (or learned some other complex activity). You had to first learn to do develop separate skills such as reading traffic signals, applying proper pressure to the pedals, using turn signals, negotiating the road, and so on. Later, as you mastered each of these skills, you then began to put them all together into one activity. As you gained experience in driving, the small tasks began to be much easier than when you first learned them. The same is true for learning how to meditate. So many times I have heard people exclaim that they have tried to meditate but they were unsuccessful. Well, if you knew nothing about driving and just got in a car one day and tried to take off down the road, I expect you would have just as much trouble learning to drive as you would trying to learn to meditate. Meditation is a complex task. It involves doing something very different than what you do throughout most of your busy and hectic days. Through meditation you must learn to relax and concentrate – no easy task for the modern person. This is why I have provided for you in this book a set of skills for you to learn separately and then put together into short easy routines. Once a solid meditation practice has been developed you should be able to go through your procedures and meditate on your chosen goal in about 20 - 30 minutes. But first, you will need to take the time and energy to learn the separate skills that will lead to the development of your complete meditation procedure. In other words, learning to meditate will take time, energy, and patience. You can find quick methods on any number of websites, magazine articles, and books but if those methods do not work for you, I encourage you to take some time to truly learn the art of meditation.

In this book I have divided the separate skills into four operations that can be learned separately and then put all together. The first operation is the Preparation. In this stage, you will create your meditation space and schedule so that you can create a regular meditation practice. The second operation is what I call The Outer Procedure. In this phase you will prepare yourself to enter into a meditative state. This step includes stretching and centering yourself so that you can begin the work of meditation. The next operation is The Inner Procedure which includes steps to prepare yourself deeply within to be ready for inner work. The final operation is the focus of meditation itself. This may sound overly complex for something that is supposed to be quite simple but doing each of these things will strengthen and deepen your practice. Each part of each procedure is a meditation exercise on its own and should be approached in that way but as you proceed through the exercises you will begin to develop a procedure that will successfully carry you from the everyday world of passing thoughts and information overload to a deep seated place of peace and inner joy. As you continue further, each operation will go from being a set of separate exercises into a complete exercise in and of itself until each operation lasts under a minute and you move quickly to a state of deep meditation.

How To Use This Book

There are several ways in which you can effectively use this book. If you are a beginner, it might be best to read through the entire book and go through the exercises sequentially. If you have some experience with meditation then you may want to look over the book and determine where you are in terms of your experience and then begin reading and working from that point. People who are experienced with meditation in general but not with Pagan meditation specifically may want to begin with the Pagan meditations in Chapter Three. Others may want to pick and choose from the exercises and the meditations provided in the text. I encourage you to discover for yourself what you need by first skimming through the book and then concentrating on the areas that may be of the most interest to you. By pursuing your own interests, I think you will eventually find yourself wanting to incorporate as much as you can into your own practice. Though the book itself describes a complete meditation procedure, not all things work for all people. As you learn and practice meditation it is my hope that you will come to develop your own procedure that works best for you. I have found, though, that it often helps to begin with a model already designed by someone else and then work from there to craft one that works for you. I offer this book to you as an example of one such model. Wherever you may choose to begin, I suggest that you do all the exercises from that point in the book at least once. If a particular exercise feels right for you then I suggest you practice that one at least two more times before moving on to the next one.

There are many different exercises and meditations in this book. They can be done by one person or by a whole class together. Most of the meditations in this book are put together in the form of a guided meditation. Each exercise lists a goal, a suggested amount of time, a suggested location, a list of needs, and a list of detailed steps. These lists help you to organize yourself before you begin the actual practice. It also helps those who may wish to lead meditation study groups.

If you plan to use this book in a group practice it will be necessary for at least one person to lead the group so that the others can just concentrate on what they are doing during the meditations. If one person does not want to do it all the time then people could switch leading the group. The leader should read through the exercise that is chosen for that session beforehand to be familiar with it and its goals. Then the leader should encourage each person to prepare themselves and take any previous steps needed to be ready for the meditation session. The leader should always remember to read aloud slowly and fully but with a soothing and calming voice. Be sure to leave time between steps for people to process what is being said and to do the activity.

This book will progress from the simple to the complex and then return you to simplicity. In the following chapter, I will introduce some very simple introductory meditations so that you can measure your current ability. Be honest with yourself in doing these exercises. If you find them easy because you have some previous experience with meditation or because you are a naturally calm and composed person then you may be able to skip some of the preparatory exercises but if you find these first few exercises difficult, then I suggest you go through all the exercises in the book. There is no shame in being an inexperienced meditator. Our society is not designed for the quietly content and joyous person. You are asked to be dissatisfied at every turn because this sense of lacking that creates a need in you. That is the need to go out and buy something that will fill that hole in your soul. We live in a capitalistic society whose purpose is to get you to buy things so that the economy will remain in growth. At every moment you are being conditioned to desire things and services so that you will spend money. Meditation is a way of breaking that conditioning. We also live in a time that is filled with constantly oncoming information. Everybody wants your attention and wants you to know their message. It is only natural that the people of such a society would have a difficult time resisting those messages and, instead, find time to be in a state of quiet and blissful peace. But, that is the purpose of meditation – to set aside a time to be at peace with yourself and the universe.

A note on the use of spiritual terms in this book: be flexible. There are as many views on the divine as there are Pagans out there and it is impossible for any author to use the specific theological language of each individual person so I hope you will translate the things I say into your own personal spiritual language and understanding. Feel free to change the words I use to represent theological concepts into the words or names that are most comfortable to you.

When Things Are Not Going Well

All developmental practices include times when things do not go well or when you feel you may not be advancing. Development is not a single straight line like a driveway. It is more like a slowly arching spiral that occasionally has dips in it. You could say it is like riding a mostly circular roller coaster. It is the same for meditation practice. As you practice, you find that you make some progress and then the progress seems to slow down or even dip a little. If you do not get too frustrated and can stay motivated then you keep practicing. Eventually, you start to make some more progress until the road turns again. What is even more crazy is that you often find the end of one path leads you back to where you started. That is the nature of a spiral – you never really get too far away from where you started. It is just that each return brings you to a slightly higher level than you were before so that you have gone nowhere and somewhere at the same time. (Spirituality is full of paradoxes.) You will have to practice for a while to experience what I mean.

All development requires having hope, faith, and love. Hope

begins the journey. You have to believe that the end of one road is a slightly better place then where you are right now. Faith gives you the strength to keep going though you are not always sure you are going in the right direction. If you walk, you will eventually get somewhere but you have to put your faith into that journey to keep going. Only when you stop will you go nowhere. Love is the journey's end. After doing all the exercises and exploring all the roads what you find at the end is the same thing that teachers and mystics have been saying for centuries. Love is where you must begin and love is where you will end. They sound like nice words but only by having the experience of pure love gained through meditation will you come to know the deep truth of those words.

If you find you are having great difficulty, then you may want to seek out a teacher or mentor. This text assumes that you do not have a mentor and that you are exploring on your own but a mentor can be useful for helping you find out where you may be stuck. I also suggest that you allow yourself to move slowly and take breaks. There is no easy and quick change to be had here; inner development takes time and patience. After doing several of these exercises I encourage you to take some time off of your practice. Mostly I suggest that you tune into what your body says. Deep inside, your body knows what is really right for you.

Exercises

I would like to introduce some very simple meditation exercises for you to try. If you find them easy to do then you may be able to skip ahead to the next chapter. If not, you should take some time to work through the exercises in this chapter.

Preliminary Exercise 1

You will need a timer with an alarm for this exercise. Begin by sitting comfortably any way that you like. Set your timer for 30 seconds and just sit. That's all – just sit. Be still and quiet until you hear the alarm go off. If that was easy try the next exercise.

Just Being

| Preliminary Exercise 2 |

Set your timer for 1 minute and do the same thing – just sit quietly. This time notice your thoughts as you sit. What did you think about in that minute? Did you feel a need to move or get up? How many different kinds of thoughts did you have? If you were able to sit for 1 minute then try the next exercise.

| Preliminary Exercise 3 |

Set your timer for 5 minutes and sit. This time, imagine that your mind is like a small child in a museum or other place where it is necessary to be quiet. Every time a thought comes into your mind politely ask the child to be quiet. Do not get upset if the child continues to make noise or even throws a fit. Remember that you love this child and would never want to hurt it. Instead of being angry, try to quietly ask the child to be silent then continue with your sitting.

Chapter One
What is Meditation?

Introduction

Before beginning a meditation practice it is important to understand what meditation actually is and, more importantly, what it is not. There are certain well documented benefits and uses for meditation but it is not a panacea for all ills. By knowing what meditation is, you can practice it to its full advantage and by knowing what it is not, you can avoid wasting precious time and energy in your practice. We will first look at how others define meditation and then I will offer my own definition. As with everything else, I hope you will work to find your own definition as well.

Defining the Term

As you might imagine, there are many different definitions for the word meditation. That is because meditation is a practice that is difficult to define and can mean many different things to many different people. Throw into the mix the different approaches and meanings that different religious practices have affixed to meditation and you get a wide variety of ideas. The true meaning of meditation is something that must be discovered by the individual practitioner but it does help to start with looking at what others have said about it. Here are some definitions of meditation as offered by some dictionaries.

The Collaborative International Dictionary of English defines meditation as:
- the act of meditating;
- close or continued thought;

- the turning or revolving of a subject in the mind;
- serious contemplation;
- reflection; and
- musing.

Word Net defines it this way:
- A continuous and profound contemplation or musing on a subject or series of subjects of a deep or abstruse nature.
- A contemplation of spiritual matters (usually on religious or philosophical subjects).

Similarly, Webster's Dictionary says that meditation directs one
- to consider thoughtfully; and
- to ponder, especially on religious matters.

While the American Heritage Dictionary of the English Language says that meditation is:
- The act or process of meditating.
- A devotional exercise of or leading to contemplation.
- A contemplative discourse, usually on a religious or philosophical subject.

The primary word used in all of these definitions is contemplation. Contemplation is deep and often prolonged thinking upon a particular subject. Some of the definitions recognize the fact that meditation is often part of a spiritual practice especially when the contemplation is on spiritual matters. I do not think, however, that mere contemplation is all that meditation is about. My experience has shown me that meditation can be a deeply moving experience that profoundly affects your spiritual practice. To find a more apt meaning of meditation we must look beyond the dictionary and look to those who have experienced and practiced meditation.

There have been many thinkers and practitioners who have offered up a definition of meditation. In an article listed on the Institute for Applied Meditation's website, for example, Puran Bair says that there are two definitions of meditation. One is "becoming aware of more of reality than that of which one is normally aware" while the second is "a rehearsal of an attitude toward life that we would like to have all the time." These are certainly different than the basic contemplation explanations offered by the dictionaries. The first of Bair's definitions implies that there is more to life than meets the eye. The person who meditates is aware of more than what the non-meditator experiences in everyday life. Through this definition we can understand that meditation can bring one to a state of heightened awareness and understanding. Surely, this is a spiritual understanding because it requires that we know and experience a connection that goes beyond the individual self. Pagans might understand this as the ability to connect to the mysterious source of all life that I call Spirit. I especially like Bair's second definition. He tells us that meditation can become a rehearsal for life. Through meditation, we can begin to visualize the type of person we want to be and then become that person. But the definition says more than that. Through meditation, we can not only develop an image of a greater self, we can also develop a greater attitude toward life that will carry us through both the good and difficult times. This definition implies that meditation is more than just a spiritual hobby. It is more than just a method of deep relaxation. It is a way to actually imagine and then create a better way of looking at and participating in life.

From a Buddhist standpoint, Joel and Michelle Levey in their book *The Fine Arts of Relaxation, Concentration, and Meditation* tell us that "meditation involves the conscious cultivation of mental qualities that enhance our understanding, power, and love, and the intentional transformation or lessening of those mind states that block these qualities." This view of meditation has some similarities to Bair's second definition above. The attitude that one needs to develop in order to create a positive way of living is created by enhancing our understanding of what life is really about, realizing our own power over our life, and engaging our love for ourselves, others, and the world. The process of developing the mind through meditation is often likened to peeling away the layers of an onion. Meditation can help us reveal the inner feelings and thoughts that underlie our actions and reactions to others bringing them out to the open light. Understanding these deep drives and desires can help us to control them and find inner peace and joy. When we peel away the outer layers of our personal defenses and fears we will eventually come to that natural inner state of peace. When that sense of inner peace is finally allowed to shine through, it will become the central focus of your life.

Lawrence LeShan in his classic book on meditation, *How To Meditate*, says that "we meditate to find, to recover, to come back to something of ourselves we once dimly and unknowingly had and have lost without knowing what it was or where or when we lost it." Similarly to the Leveys' definition, LeShan's statement says that we have a deeper truth hiding within ourselves and that meditation can help us to reveal it. Though Levey implies that what we may discover within the self is something wonderful and new, LeShan claims that what we find through meditation is something we once had but lost. Many mystics claim that children are naturally born with the sense of wonder, awe, joy, and play that are the essential elements of a spiritual life but that as they grow into adulthood they lose those qualities. Is it that as we grow up we come to terms with the harshness of life and lose our sense of joy or is it that we are born with a sense of universal wonder and a joyous nature and it is the development of our own intellect that eventually supplants that joy with constant fear and doubt? Whatever it is, LeShan says that we lose it without even knowing it and that meditation can help us to retrieve it so that we may again live in peace and joy.

In his book *Meditation: The Inner Way*, Naomi Humphrey states that "meditation can be thought of as pure perception or total awareness." This is similar to Bair's first definition. Through meditation we become more aware of ourselves and the world we live in. However, Humphrey claims that this perception is pure and the awareness total. This is an even greater degree of realization than declared by Bair. Humphrey states that this perception allows us to see all things succinctly through a clear and concise understanding of the world. This is more than just awareness - this is a deep understanding of the mysteries of life. When one sees all things clearly there is no need for fear or doubt and a purpose and place in life is identified. Such a person has no need to hide interior motivations. All becomes clear and the mind and heart can take solace in this understanding. Humphrey implies that this total awareness is a good thing – that someone who knows about life and who can clearly observe it does so with a sense of calm and comfort. Only a world that is essentially full of peace and joy can offer that type of calmness and Humphrey seems to be saying that this type of peaceful and wondrous existence is at the heart of what we find in a state of total awareness discovered through meditation. All these definitions offer something distinctively different from those proposed by the dictionary meanings of the word meditation. The definitions from the actual practitioners and teachers of meditation emphasis that it develops a recovery of the true self – the self that understands its connection to the universe. The term most often used is *awareness* and is modified as *expanded awareness*.

For my own definition I have chosen to look at the word *meditation* itself. It has two parts: "medi" and "tate." The first part ("medi") means to be in the middle of something. Take the word <u>medi</u>ate, for example, which means to attempt to find the common ground or middle way between two or more differing opinions. The <u>Medi</u>terranean Sea used to be considered the middle of the earth which is literally what its name means "medi" + "terrain". The word <u>medi</u>um indicates something between two extremes. The second part of the word meditate ("tate") is similar to the word "state" which means to stand or to set into position. To resusci<u>tate</u> means to bring back to a state of health. To irri<u>tate</u> someone is to put him or her in a state of excitement. To levi<u>tate</u> is to put a body in a position above the ground. To meditate, then, would mean to put someone in a state between something else. What are these two states? Again, this is where your spiritual understanding must come into play. I believe meditation puts you into a state between the pure energy of Spirit and the mundane life. As living creatures we cannot actually become pure Spirit – that only happens after death. We can, however, attempt to reach a place that is between the consciousness of everyday living and the peaceful abundant stillness of Spirit. Pure Spirit is the source of all peace and beauty (as well as their opposites) and we can get a glimpse of those things when we meditate. When we consciously take on this practice we are developing an awareness of the presence of Spirit in our lives and we learn to use that energy to deepen our faith and strengthen our lives. My own definition of meditation, then, is

> *I believe meditation puts you into a state between the pure energy of Spirit and the mundane life.*

that it is a state of highly focused awareness capable of creating a profound sense of inner peace and joy through a connection to Spirit.

As you can see, there are many varied definitions of the term meditation and that is as it should be for meditation is a highly personal experience creating as many definitions as there are practitioners. As you begin and develop your meditation practice, I hope that you will take these definitions to heart but that you will also be open to developing your own definition as well. More importantly, however, is to not let a written definition define for you what meditation *should* be. Let your higher self guide you as you practice and be open to whatever experience may come your way regardless of whether or not it fits into a written definition. Being in a state between the here and now and the timeless energy of the universe should certainly bring about new learning and life experiences that words may not adequately convey. Only if you are open to those possibilities will you be able to experience them.

Now that we have explored several meanings for the word meditation, let us take a chance to look at what meditation is not. Sometimes a definition for a thing becomes understood even more closely when you also know what that same thing is not. There are many mistaken notions about meditation. For one, people assume that meditation is a type of cure-all for all types of illnesses or personality disorders. This is not the case. Though meditation is a useful tool for good health it is but one of many such tools. Pagans know intimately the connection between body and mind and how important mental attitude can be towards maintaining good health but to assume that one type of practice alone will lead to perfect health is not a wise attitude. Sometimes meditation can actually aggravate certain conditions – especially mental ones - because the process can involve delving deeply into the inner self. The deep recesses of the mind can hide many demons and fears and it takes a certain amount of strength and centered-ness to be able to deal with these things. If you are not certain yourself that you are prepared to deal with these kinds of inner workings then I urge you to find a meditation teacher or partner – someone that can work with you to help you wrangle with these inner demons successfully.

Meditation will not turn you into an instant guru. Unfortunately, there are those who practice meditation just so that they can tell others that they practice meditation. It is assumed that by simply making that statement that someone can announce to the world their superior spiritual station in life. You can compare learning to meditate to learning to play the guitar. To play basic chords on a guitar is a skill that most people can master in a few lessons but to truly play guitar with skill involves learning complex chords, scales, strumming patterns, and so on. Both a beginning guitar player and a more advanced player can say with honesty that they can play the guitar without necessarily identifying how well and consistently they play but it is quite obvious the difference in ability when the playing begins. Meditation is also a developed skill. There are many who can sit down in a curious posture and be quiet for a few minutes and then proclaim that he or she is a meditator and, thus, obviously a superior being, but developing a truly effective and worthwhile practice takes time and patience. If it is more important to you to claim to others that you meditate in order to seem more spiritual than it is for you to actually devote years of practice to become a skilled meditator, then little will come of whatever practice you do. Just because you meditate, and the practice reveals to you all sorts of wonderful insights, and you even develop a profound sense of inner peace, you will still not be a better, more important, or more spiritual person than anyone else. You will, however, find a better way to live your own life. Boasting to others about your meditation expertise does nothing more than boost your own individual ego and may even become yet another block to get in the way of overcoming that ego which is one of the goals of meditation and of any true spiritual practice.

Another important distinction is that meditation practice is not the experience of meditation itself. The meditative experience is not the sitting or the quiet or the space you are in. It is the experience of the interior reality. Think of a hot air balloon. It carries you in a small basket up into the sky lifted by hot gases contained in the balloon. As you climb into the sky you experience the feeling of being free and soaring above the objects and people on the ground. The sensation may be exhilarating or frightening to you. Either way, the balloon is not the experience – it is only the vehicle for the experience. In the same way meditation is the vehicle and not the experience.

Most of all, meditation is not easy nor is it hard. On the surface, it does seem easy. There are several meditation teachers who

Just Being

will tell you that the instructions are simple enough. To meditate you simply sit. That's it – just sit! Ah, but if that is all there was to it then there wouldn't need to be all those books out there directing people on how to meditate. How many books have you seen that tell you about how to put your body in a chair? Not too many because everyone knows how to do that – you just plop your body down – but meditation involves more than just sitting down. There's the little problem of what to do while you are just sitting. Just sit means to not move, not think, not process the endless amount of information, worries, deliberations, or musings that go through our head at every minute of every day. Our minds are always in constant motion even when we sleep. To just focus our thinking for even a short amount of time is a very challenging task indeed – especially for us over-active over-achieving Westerners. Just sitting is more than just sitting and learning even this basic requirement of meditation takes time, patience, and a commitment. But in the end, meditation *is* simple. It *is* just sitting. It all depends on how easy just sitting is for you.

Why Meditate?

At this point you may be asking: well, if meditation is so difficult, why should I even bother trying to learn how to do it? The answer is that like learning to play an instrument or developing any other skill there are some definite rewards to putting in the time. People have different reasons for wanting to learn meditation and sometimes the result they achieve may be different than the original goal. The goal that most people have when they first begin meditating is to find a sense of inner peace or to seek better health. Other people use meditation for religious purposes like seeking the presence of a divine being or to connect to the higher self. In Eastern religions where meditation is an integral part of the spiritual practice, the goal of meditation is often to seek enlightenment. To be enlightened is to see the world clearly – free of all desires and social messages – and to see the true essence of the self. By seeking enlightenment, some Eastern religions say, one breaks the cycle of death and rebirth and enters into a blissful state of non-being. All of these things are worthwhile goals for the practice of meditation because it has been shown to demonstrate many positive effects for the mind, heart, body, and soul.

    The positive effects of a continued meditation practice to the body include developing a decreased metabolic rate, a lower blood pressure, a lower heart rate, lower levels of stress, and an improved air flow to the lungs. Mentally, a consistent meditation practice has been shown to decrease anxiety, depression, and moodiness and can improve your learning ability and memory. Emotionally, you may be able to better learn to control emotions and face difficult feelings. Meditation can also help you to develop self-acceptance and a heightened self-awareness. A devoted meditation practice can also develop spiritual growth. This type of growth happens when you find a deeper connection to self, others, and to the universe and when you connect to Spirit.

    It should be mentioned that there can be some negative experiences associated with a meditation practice and that if any of these things are experienced, you should seek out some help from an experienced teacher before going any further. Remember that meditation can cause you to look deep within yourself and experience a connection with the universe. Both of these experiences can be confusing and even frightening if not approached with an open mind and a calm centered disposition. These experiences can cause some to become depressed or to even become struck with panic or anxiety brought on by confusion and disorientation. Another possible and often experienced negative effect is to experience tension or pain in the body from remaining in a single position for a long time. These effects can be lessened by stretching the body and by finding subtle ways to relieve or even ignore the temporary discomfort. Never, of course, put your body in a position to cause it permanent damage such as might be done by bending or twisted broken or damaged parts of the body. Since meditation can affect your body and your health, your medical practitioner should be consulted before beginning a practice - especially if you have a specific mental or physical problem that may be affected by your regular practice.

    The negative effects mentioned here are real but should not dissuade you from trying meditation for yourself. The key is to remain calm and to be open throughout your sessions and not be afraid of what you may experience. If you experience any negative effect then stop your session and seek out the professional assistance of someone who can help you make sense of what you experienced.

What Happens In Meditation?

Most texts on meditation explain it as an activity primarily of the mind. There are active meditations and there are passive meditations. In a passive meditation, the body is still and the focus is on what goes on in the head. I think meditation should involve the whole self, however. To explain what I mean I often use a symbol called the equilateral cross. It is a symbol containing four arms of equal size radiating from a center and ending in a circle and has been used by Masons, Native Americans, the Celts and many others as a powerful sacred symbol. This sign is also a map of the universe as well as a map of the self because there is no separation or difference between the macrocosmic (the universe) and the microcosmic (the self). This is the meaning of the term from the Emerald Tablet "As above, so below."

Illustration 1: The Equilateral Cross

Each of the four arms represents one of the four elements (Earth, Air, Fire, and Water) and the four directions - the macrocosm - but can also represent one of the four parts of the self (Body, Mind, Heart, and Soul) or the microcosm. The outer circle which brings together the four elements into a unified whole represents Spirit. The symbol of the equilateral cross is significant for it visually represents that all four parts of each of these things is equal to the other and that they are all part of one whole (the circle). My reason for explaining all this is to claim that studying the effect of meditation on only one part of the self is not sufficient. We need to see how it affects every part of the self.

Meditation affects the body by encouraging relaxation. The results of this are usually a deeper rate of breathing, a slower heart rate, and muscles that release tension. In turn, these actions can stimulate other relaxation responses throughout the body including the reduction of chemicals that are produced during moments of stress. The effects of stress are not, in and of themselves, harmful. It is the duration of stress that causes harm. Our bodies are built to handle stress in moderate doses but are greatly challenged by a constant onslaught of stressors. Meditation can help reverse those pressures on the body and can return us to a state of calm and relaxed awareness. Although I have found little research on the idea of levels of physical relaxation, I would like to suggest that we can experience at least five which I have listed in the chart below. One way to monitor your stress level is through your heart rate but an even easier way is to monitor your breathing.

Level	Name	Characteristic	Breath
One	High Tension	A state of of fight or flight readiness	Very shallow
Two	Low Tension	A state of moderate stress and fixed attention	Shallow
Three	Moderate Relaxation	Most muscles loose and at rest	Slow
Four	Deep Relaxation	All muscles very loose, no tension	Very slow
Five	Intense Relaxation	A loss of sensations of self	Very full

Illustration 2: Levels of Physical Relaxation

Meditation affects the mind by altering brain wave activity. As we think and go through the day, our brains operate with different electrical wave patterns. Like currents on a calm lake, these patterns ebb and flow in regular cycles called peaks and troughs. The speed at which these patterns repeat is called the brain wave frequency and is often represented as a wave pattern. The most basic wave pattern is called a sine wave which looks like the illustration below.

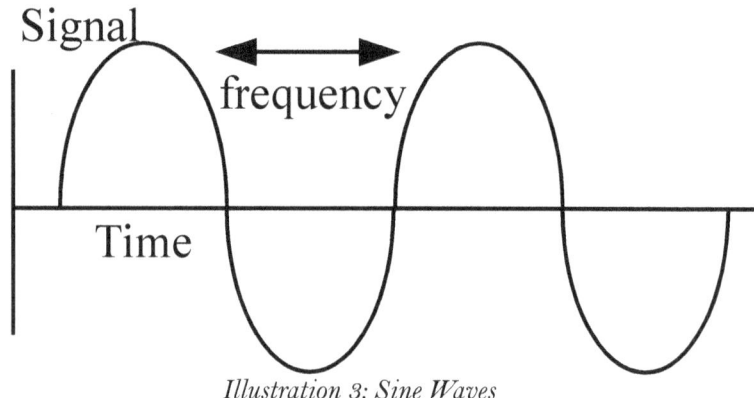

Illustration 3: Sine Waves

Frequencies are rated in Herz (Hz) which measures the number of peaks per minute. A sine wave measured at 2 Hz means that 2 peaks of the wave appear every minute. The frequency rates of our thoughts affect how we think and researchers have identified five mental states directly related to the range of our brain wave patterns. The five states and their signal rates are illustrated in the following chart.

Level	Name	Wave Rate	Experience
One	Gamma	26 – 100 Hz	Hyperactive: very active thought and fear states
Two	Beta	12 - 25 Hz	Active: busy with day to day thoughts
Three	Alpha	8 to 12 Hz	Relaxed: daydream-like but also alert
Four	Theta	4 to 8 Hz	Light Trance: normal light sleep or quiet
Five	Delta	Less than 4 Hz	Deep Trance: deep sleep or intense peace

Illustration 4: Brain Wave Patterns

Researchers have discovered that the state of meditation

actually involves activating several brain wave patterns at once. In effect, the mind goes into a deep sleep state yet there is still an awareness. Deep meditation involves using brain wave patterns from the Alpha, Theta, and Delta levels. The effect of meditation on the mind, then, is to reach a level of awareness that includes a sense of deep peace and silence.

You may notice that there are some similarities between the five physical states of relaxation and the five states of brain wave activity. Without a doubt, the mind and body influence each other but their states do not always coincide. It is possible to have a physically relaxed body but a very active mind. One of the challenges of meditation is to seek complete relaxation. It is fairly easy to coax the body into a moderately relaxed state and appear to be, in fact, relaxed but the mind may not always follow suit.

Meditation also affects the heart or the emotional side of the self. Through the emotions, we learn to love and accept ourselves and others and to develop ways to deal with each other. Our emotions can range from utter hatred to an unconditional love and from desperate fear to a sense of tranquil joy. Emotions can be useful in helping us to assess particular situations and determine an adequate response. We need love to form relationships and we need fear to have the energy to escape from life threatening situations. Sometimes, though, emotions can get in the way of acting rationally and reasonably. Emotions need to be linked to thoughtfulness so that the consequences of possible actions can be assessed. Meditation can help us to observe and moderate our emotions so that we can go through life on a more even keel. Certainly, we do not want to eliminate emotions from life experience. Pagans celebrate the great passion and joy of life but sometimes we can learn to avoid the painful results of rash actions fueled by powerful unbridled emotions. Emotions also have an effect on how we view the world and life. Without some emotions, life can seem to be dull and, well, lifeless. Emotional development can help us to appreciate life more fully. Through meditation it is possible to learn to observe and control personal emotional reactions. More importantly, meditation can help you reach a higher level of emotional growth that allows you to accept yourself and all others.

The psychologist, Kazimierz Dabrowski, developed a theory of emotional development he called "positive disintegration." The idea is that people go through stages of emotional growth that range from strong self-centeredness to a sense of unity with all beings. In effect, the personal ego goes through a disintegration on its way to developing a more universal identification. He lists five stages of emotional development that are encountered on the way. In order to make these levels easier to comprehend, I am listing them according to changes in personal values and identification.

Level	Name	Personal Values	Identification
One	Primary Integration	None – often supplied by an authority	Self only
Two	Unilevel Disintegration	Very basic- influenced from a group or group leader	As part of a group
Three	Spontaneous Multilevel Disintegration	Higher values developed but are flexible and unstable – often developed from written sources	As a part of the world but often conflicted between self and others
Four	Directed Multilevel Disintegration	Stable higher values developed from personal experience	Universal with empathy for others and unconditional love for close people
Five	Secondary Integration	Higher universal values embraced	Unconditional love for all beings

Illustration 5: Levels of Emotional Growth

It is interesting to note that Dabrowski believed that depression and confusion were natural parts of the growth process of developing higher values and a wider range of emotional acceptance. Instead of viewing these things as negative and detrimental, he sees them as important steps to a better self. We have already seen that some negative states can be brought on through meditation but it may be that these are not unfortunate interferences but can be, instead, part of the process of finding, accepting, and developing the inner self.

The soul can also go through levels of development brought on by meditation. The practice of meditation can help you deepen connections between yourself, others, and can help you to feel that you are an important part of the world and universe in which you live. In her grand and expansive book, *Mysticism: The Nature and Development of Spiritual Consciousness*, Evelyn Underhill outlines five stages of spiritual development. She based her research for the book on the works of several (mostly Christian) mystics. I will explain the levels in Pagan terms, however.

Level	Name	Characteristic
One	Awakening	One gets a glimpse of Spirit and desires to break from self-centeredness
Two	Purification	One attempts to cleanse body, mind, heart, and soul to prepare for deeper connections
Three	Illumination	One feels a connection to Spirit and experiences that connection through cosmic forces or deities
Four	Dark Night of the Soul	The soul desires to unite with Spirit but the body, mind, and heart become exhausted. A time of doubt and resistance is encountered.
Five	Union	One breaks through the cloud of fear and becomes directly united with Spirit.

Illustration 6: Levels of Spiritual Growth

There are some interesting similarities between the levels of emotional and spiritual development. As with Dobrowski, Underhil also believes that negative states are part of growth. Her fourth level (the Dark Night of the Soul which is a title she borrowed from St. John of the Cross) is recognized as a time of darkness and depression-like feelings. Again, these may not be undesirable conditions. They are an essential part of the conditions for growth. Another important similarity is the comparison of the concepts of identification (emotional growth) and connection (spiritual growth). Through your heart you can identify with others to create conditions of sympathy and empathy. Through your soul you can make a connection with Spirit. At the highest emotional level you can identify with Spirit but only through the soul can you make an actual connection. The difference between the two is that with an identity there is still a sense of "me." You can identify with something but doing so does not necessarily create a relationship. It is through your soul that you make an actual connection. The energy of Spirit is what makes you alive and when that energy is opened to another being, you have a connection. The highest connection, of course, is with Spirit itself.

It is no accident that there are five levels for each of the four parts of the self. I consciously chose the theories of those who identified with five levels so that I could make an easy comparison between them all and with the elements. The number of levels really is not significant because levels do not actually come in numerical packets. Nature knows no straight lines or square boxes. Development and progression take place on a gradual spectrum but charts and graphs can help us to get a snapshot of where we are. It's like adding a grid to a map. The lines are not real but they can help us to agree on locations for quick reference. Levels can be identified through 3, 5, or 12, numbers or through any number of subdivisions. Five does seem to be a popular number, though. That being said, let us compare all the levels with what we have observed so far.

Level	Body	Mind	Heart	Soul
One	High Tension	Hyperactive	Self Identification	Awakening
Two	Low Tension	Active	Group Identification	Purification
Three	Moderate Relaxation	Relaxed	Conflicted Identification	Illumination
Four	Deep Relaxation	Light Trance	Worldly Identification	Dark Night
Five	Intense Relaxation	Deep Trance	Universal Identification	Union

Illustration 7: Comparison of Levels

From this chart you can see that there are five levels of the self each of which is a higher level of awareness. One can progress from a state of high mental activity and tension where the focus is strictly on the self and on one's own experiences of the divine toward a state of deep relaxation with a quiet mind where one embraces all life and all experiences to a point where that person is actually united with the pure beauty and love of Spirit. The progression for the body and the mind is to come to a point where one can release the concept and experience of the single self and become part of the greater self of Spirit. This all makes complete sense if you understand the relationship of the four elements and the four parts of the self to each other and to material and non-material reality.

In Hermetic philosophy, the universe was created through the elements. The theory goes that beyond the realm of the stars is the realm of the Divine fiery water. Here, Fire and Water are combined to represent the pure essence of Spirit. For Spirit to become manifest and create the universe the fiery water divides. Fire becomes the sun or the masculine force and Water becomes the moon or the feminine force of creation. These two separate elements create Eden which in Hebrew means the vapor - Air. Air is the breath that contains the seeds of matter (dust) which forms Earth and, subsequently, life. Thus, Spirit becomes matter by progressing through the four elements.

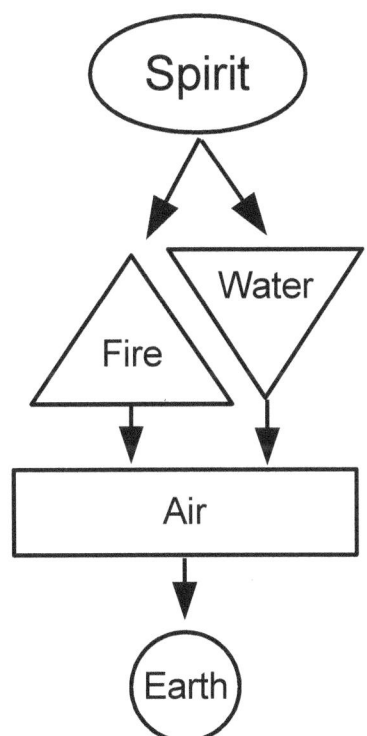

Illustration 8: A Hermetic Cosmogony of the Elements

In this description of the elements, Spirit moves from energy to matter in stages - each one being more dense than the previous until Earth and all life is created. Creation moves from being totally non-material (energy) to becoming material (matter). This is too

Just Being

simplistic, of course, because all life and all creation is in constant flux so that all things change and nothing is completely devoid of Spirit but a rough representation of the process can be seen below.

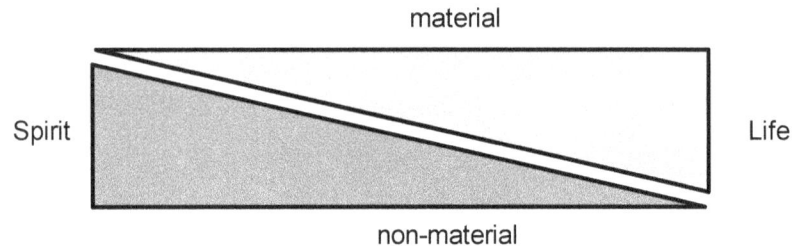

Illustration 9: The Non-Material to The Material

The same holds true for the progression of the four parts of the self toward Spirit which is the goal of meditation. Each part of the self moves from material (self) to the non-material (Spirit). By focusing on each part of the self, a total progression can be made.

It is interesting to note that the self also demonstrates a progression of material to less material. The body is the physical part of the self and it is the most material. The mind is less so. We know that the mind has a material connection to the part of the body we call the brain but the brain is not all there is to the mind. The mind includes all our thoughts which are not purely material but are partially electrical energy and the ideas that spark them are not so easy to identify as material. Our minds are a combination of material and non-material. Our hearts are even less connected to the material. Even though we speak of feeling from the heart we do not actually mean the organ of the body called the heart. The only purpose of the physical heart is to pump blood throughout the body but because blood goes to all parts of the body and because we feel emotions throughout the body we say that emotions come from the heart. In reality, however, emotions are non-material energy patterns and the "heart" is less materially based than the mind. The soul, of course, is the least materially based part of the self since it is a spark of the full Spirit.

Chapter One

Material	>>>>>>		Non-Material
V V V V	Element	Part of Self	Ultimate Goal
	Earth	Body	Intense Relaxation
	Air	Mind	Awareness of Deep Peace
	Fire	Heart	Universal Identification
	Water	Soul	Union
Non-Material	Spirit		

Illustration 10: Progression of the Parts of Self

This movement from material to non-material, then, is the desired progression for meditation and should be what happens when you learn to practice meditation consistently and effectively. You begin with the body and strive for a sense of complete relaxation. Next, you clear and quiet the mind slowing down your brain wave patterns until you can enter a state of awareness and deep silence. After that, you open your heart to embrace yourself and all other beings until you enter a state of complete loving-kindness which then allows you to connect to all things and become in union with the universe. All of this takes place within the self though nothing may appear to be happening from the outside. Just sitting is not just sitting.

Types of Meditation

Many different types of meditation have been developed over the course of history. Different spiritual traditions that use meditation have developed practices that support their own theological positions. Many of the meditation methods historically developed have focused on developing one part of the self. Some focus on the body while others center on developing the mind, the heart, or the soul. There are several methods that affect two or more parts of the self but tend to have a main focus on one. There are also meditations that involve movement. Up to now we have been discussing mostly passive forms of meditation – ones that involve remaining in one physical position for some time - but meditation can also take place while the body is in motion. This type of meditation is called active meditation and is very challenging because it requires a constantly relaxed body, a mind that is focused solely on the activity, a heart that stays open without judging the events happening, and a soul that can stay connected. It is these things which make an activity a meditation and not just another aimless motion.

In addition to the many types of meditation, there are also several methods for getting someone into a state of meditation. I would like to identify three types: *guided, focused,* and *unfocused.* Guided meditation is directed by someone other than the meditator. The guide often follows some sort of meditation script that leads others into a meditative state and through a meditative journey. Focused meditation is done by the meditator and has some sort of central goal for that meditation session. That focus is usually based upon one of the four parts of the self – most often the mind. Unfocused meditation is usually done alone and has no central focus at all. It is a completely open form of meditation and is often the most difficult. Below I will list several types of meditations based on the four parts of the self and the kind of meditations that can be done using the three methods.

Physical Meditations

Guided:
Dances of Peace, Tai Chi, Gi Gong, Yoga

Focused:
Mindfulness, Energy or other types of healing, Relaxation, Stretching

Unfocused:
Art, Walking meditation, Sexual meditations, Bodily Sensation Awareness

Most physical meditations are active meditations. They involve movement of all or parts of the body. One exception to this is when one does a sitting meditation but focuses on relaxing the body. Though I list physical meditations first, I believe that you should practice and develop your skills in sitting meditation before you apply those practices to moving meditations. Guided physical meditations include dancing such as those done by the group The Universal Dances of Peace. These are usually simple dance forms with chants that are inspired or influenced by many different cultures. Someone guides you through the dance steps and the chant but eventually these are drawn into the self and the group dances together. Tai Chi is another effective form of movement meditation. Specific movements are taught and done in a slow and deliberate way. The movements are often connected to the breath and to the concept of "Chi" which make them very powerful. Gi Gong is similar to Tai Chi except that it focuses on movements that are done standing still while Tai Chi practitioners tend to move in many directions across the space. Yoga was originally meant to prepare Indian meditators by stretching their bodies so that they could sit for long periods of time. Eventually, Yoga developed into its own kind of meditation. Practitioners focus on physical sensations as they stretch and adopt forms of deep breathing to connect them to their body. Actually I am speaking here of one kind of Yoga called Hatha Yoga which focuses on the body and is the form of Yoga people most people know. There are really four kinds of Yoga each of which fits into the four categories I have already discussed. Patanjali in his text on Yoga ("The Yoga Sutras") was one of the first to recognize that different forms of meditation relate to different people. People who are physical relate well to more physical forms of meditation, etc.

Physical forms of meditation that are not guided but have an internal focus include mindfulness, healing meditations, and relaxation exercises. Mindfulness is a very powerful form of meditation and one of the most popular writers on the practice is the Buddhist writer Thich Nhat Hanh. He describes the process of mindfulness as doing any common activity but with a clear mind that is focused strictly on the activity itself and nothing else. It is a challenging but rewarding practice. Popular activities for practicing mindfulness include gardening and crafting. Healing which involves working with another body can be another form of movement meditation. Here, the focus is on sending healing and loving energy to someone else.

Unfocused physical meditation can come in many forms. Art is a particularly strong way in which one can be involved in meditative unfocused movement. Visual art, free dancing, and improvisatory drumming are just some of many ways that you can allow yourself to move creatively but with an open mind. Walking is another popular type of movement meditation. Buddhists use a form of slow deliberate walking for meditation. Walking a special sacred space like a labyrinth or even hiking a mountain if done in a clear meditative state of mind can be powerful. Hands can be used for meditation in practices such as counting beads on a prayer necklace while repeating sacred phrases and the whole body can be part of a meditative activity such as in the practice of sacred sex.

Mental Meditations

Guided:
Visualizations

Focused:
Visual, Sound, Symbolic, Thought (koan) or Phrase (mantra)

Unfocused:
Contemplative Reading, Lucid Dreaming, Free Visualization

      Most meditation techniques focus on the mind. There are many guided mental meditations which usually involve creating visualizations in the mind. There are also literally hundreds of focused meditations all which attempt to focus the mind on one particular subject so that all other thoughts cease. These objects of focus can be visual, aural, symbolic, or even a particularly chosen thought or question. Visual objects that are often chosen are candles, spiritual artwork such as a mandala, or religious symbols or objects. In each case, the meditator stares at the object while attempting to focus all attention upon it until all other thoughts are cleared away. Sound, too, can be a mental focus. Certain types of music, repeated chants, or audible phrases can focus the mind on a single objective. Another type of mental meditation is to focus on a particular thought or question. Focusing on a question is a Zen tradition where a very difficult problem is posed to the student (called a koan) and the meditation takes place as the student puts all of his or her attention on finding the answer to that problem. An example of a typical koan is "What was your original face look like before you were born?" or "What is your true essence?" This type of intense concentration on a question or thought – especially a spiritual thought – is also known as the practice of contemplation.

There are also several kinds of unfocused meditations for the mind. One is contemplative reading in which one reads sacred poetry or writing and then allows the mind to contemplate on certain aspects of what is read. It is similar to the focused practice of contemplation except that the reading is used to guide the mind, which remains open to the ideas that may arise from what is read. A free visualization is another form of unfocused meditation.

Emotional Meditations

Guided:
Loving-Kindness, Relationship Visualizations

Focused:
Devotions

Unfocused:
Sensation Awareness

Emotional meditations focus on what we call the "heart" though that is a misnomer. What we mean to say is that emotional meditation focuses on the part of ourselves that accepts and embraces ourselves and others. To understand what complete emotional acceptance means it is important to understand the different spheres of relationships. There are at least four that can be counted: the self, others, the world, and the cosmos.

Just Being

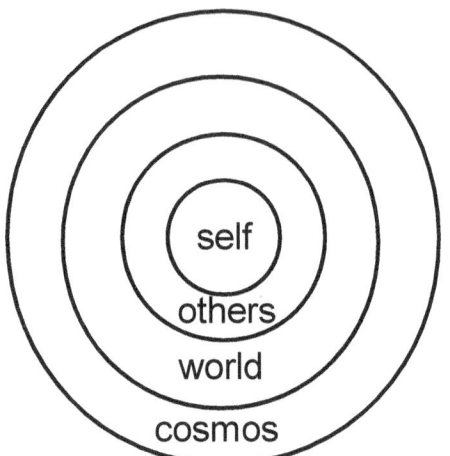

Illustration 11: The Spheres of Relationships

    In the diagram above, each sphere represents a circle of relationship for ourselves. You stand at the very center of the circle. The closest relationship to you is yourself. Next is your relationship to others. The next farthest relationship is with the world and then the cosmos. It is easier to relate to ourselves than it is to relate to the whole universe but a universal connection is possible. Each of these spheres, of course, could be subdivided into more levels. For example, you could divide the sphere of the world into personal relationships, family, close friends, acquaintances and so on. By the cosmos I mean that sense of complete unity of all things visible and invisible and includes our relationship with Spirit.

    One kind of practice that is useful in reaching these relationship levels is the Buddhist practice of the Loving-Kindness Meditation where the practitioner extends feelings of love and acceptance to all the levels of relationships. Other types of emotional meditations use visualizations to achieve a similar effect. Often, though, the visualizations focus on only one relational sphere at a time. A focused emotional meditation can be done by concentrating on devoting one's love and life to a deity or spiritual concept. An unfocused emotional meditation can be done when the meditator simply attempts to experience whatever feelings arise within the self.

Chapter One

Spiritual Meditations

all types:
Absorption

Spiritual meditations take place when the meditator becomes completely absorbed in a particular focus. Any of the above meditations can become spiritual if, in the process of doing them, one becomes so involved with the meditation that one is absorbed into it and no longer feels a separation between the self and the rest of the universe. This is called Absorption and is the highest form of any meditative practice. Nearly all religious practices that use meditation emphasize that the goal of any deep practice is to escape the ego and become connected to the ultimate reality of the universe.

The Stages of Meditation

In this text, I will present to you a system of meditation that will involve all four parts of the self while also allowing for the flexibility to maintain a particular focus or goal for the meditator. To do that, we will need to develop a meditative procedure that includes the whole self. This procedure will progress from the material to the non-material or from the body to the soul each of which will have a specific goal. I will do this by helping you to develop both an Inner Procedure and an Outer Procedure. The Outer Procedure will prepare your whole self for going into a meditative state. The Inner Procedure will access the deeper parts of your self so that you can focus on your goal.

Part of the Self	Goal
Body	Relaxation
Mind	Concentration
Heart	Acceptance
Soul	Absorption

Illustration 12: Meditative Goals

These goals and the central focus of your meditation will

become the stages of your meditative practice. You will learn to develop each stage separately at first so that you can fully develop your ability with each goal. Then you will learn to combine these stages to create a powerful and complete meditative method.

Summary

In this chapter I have shared with you my idea that meditation is a state between daily life and the ultimate peace and joy of Spirit and that in that state one develops a highly focused degree of awareness wherein that joy and peace can be experienced personally. Though people have many different reasons for practicing meditation and though it can have a variety of benefits, I believe that meditation is essentially a spiritual practice. Since my theological perspective of life is Pagan, I am approaching the meditation process primarily as a Pagan spiritual practice. That approach means developing a meditative practice that includes all four parts of the self (related to the four elements) rather than on just one part of the self because meditation can have a positive effect on each of these parts and on developing the self as a whole. Developing the whole self and connecting with Spirit are the goals for the type of practice I will explain in this text.

Exercises

In this section and in subsequent chapters I will offer to you a variety of exercises or meditation practices. I suggest you try each one and repeat any that you find effective.

Exercise 1.1 – Just Sitting

Begin your first exercise by just sitting. There is no other goal at this point. Just sit. You don't have to be stiff or uncomfortable but do try not to move excessively. Just sit still for at least 10 seconds. You can try counting slowly from 1 to 10 in your mind. It does not matter at all what you think about in those 10 seconds. All you need to do is sit still.

Chapter One

Exercise no.	1 (1.1)
Goal	To begin to learn how to meditate
Minimum time	10 seconds
Location	anywhere
Needs	none
Steps	
1. Find a comfortable place to sit. 2. Sit for at least 10 seconds. 3. End your meditation.	

Exercise 1.2 – Just Breathing

In this exercise you are asked to simply pay attention to your breathing. You do not need to alter your breath. Just follow it as it goes in and out of your body for at least 10 seconds.

Exercise no.	2 (1.2)
Goal	To follow your breathe
Minimum length of time	10 seconds
Location	anywhere
Steps	
1. Sit comfortably 2. Pay attention to your breathing for at least 10 seconds. 3. End your meditation.	

Exercise 1.3 – 15 Second Meditation

Use the technique of following the breath for the next three exercises. Each one will be based on a slight increase of time.

Exercise no.	3 (1.3)
Goal	To sit for 15 seconds.
Minimum length of time	15 seconds
Location	anywhere
Needs	none
Steps	

1. Sit comfortably
2. Sit quietly for at least 15 seconds following your breath.
3. End your meditation.

Exercise 1.4 – 30 Second Meditation

Do the same thing for at least 30 seconds.

Exercise no.	4 (1.4)
Goal	To sit for at least 30 seconds.
Minimum length of time	30 seconds
Location	anywhere
Needs	none
Steps	

1. Sit comfortably
2. Sit quietly for at least 30 seconds following your breath.
3. End your meditation.

Chapter One

Exercise 1.5 – 1 Minute Meditation

Exercise no.	5 (1.5)
Goal	To sit for at least one minute
Minimum length of time	one minute
Location	anywhere
Needs	none
Steps	

1. Sit comfortably.
2. Sit for at least one minute following your breath.
3. End your meditation.

Just Being

Chapter Two
How To Meditate
(The Outer Procedure)

Introduction

In this chapter, we will take a look at the actual mechanics of how you can learn to develop your own Pagan meditation practice by developing what I call the Outer Procedure. You will learn how to prepare yourself for meditation and then study the different parts of creating a complete procedure. I recommend that you develop a routine that you do as a regular part of your practice. This procedure will insure that you include all parts of the self in your meditation and will help to bring your body, mind, heart, and soul into a state of readiness for your meditative work. I view meditation much in the same light that I do ritual. For each, there are steps to take to prepare yourself and your space and there is a procedure that brings you into deeper state of consciousness that allows you to practice your work. There is a sacred connection made between the person doing the ritual and the energies of the universe. A successful ritual requires learning how to do each part of the ritual separately and then bringing those parts together into a single whole. The meditation procedure is also about learning separate parts that are weaved together to create a whole process. We will go over each of the separate parts first so that you can learn to do each well. Then, you will be encouraged to develop your own routine and work on it until it becomes a seamless and integrated procedure that will prepare you for the inner work ahead.

Reasons for Disappointment

If you had trouble doing any of the preliminary exercises in the first chapter, do not feel bad. Most people have a difficult time sitting quietly. I have designed the Inner and Outer Procedures to help people focus themselves so that they can meditate better. Before working on a procedure, however, it may be helpful to be aware of some of the pitfalls that may come up during a practice which can make meditation challenging. By knowing about these possibilities ahead of time you may be able to avoid them. Though there may be as many reasons for failure as there are meditators, there are three main pitfalls that each person should be careful to avoid in their meditation practice. Those three are: encountering distractions, developing unclear goals, and having a lack of persistence.

If you consider that many of us are always on the go and that information comes at us at all times and all places, it is not hard to understand why we can easily become distracted. Meditation, however, requires concentration and distraction is the enemy of concentration. There are many different kinds of distraction. Physical distractions include pains, itches, minor discomforts, twitches, or desires. There are some some schools of meditation which recommend that you do not move at all during a meditation practice. I do not concur with this idea although I understand its intention. The concept is that if you give in to any distraction at all, you will be delayed in seeking that deeper state of meditation which is the ultimate goal. I think it is much easier to go ahead and scratch that itch or adjust that sitting position if doing so provides some relief and allows the meditator to return to his or her focus. If, however, the itches and pains continue to the point where they become a long string of continuous distractions then it may be time to consider ignoring them instead. The idea is to stay focused and you have to decide what is the best way for you to do that. It is common to experience some muscular twitches while sitting. These are often the result of muscles releasing energy as you relax. These are best ignored if possible. Just allow your muscles to relax naturally and these should go away in time. Stretching before meditation can also help you to avoid twitches.

Desires can also be an annoying source of distraction and there are many kinds of desires. While sitting, you may become hungry or thirsty. If you are not used to sitting still for long periods of time your body will try to find things to do by initiating desires. It is also possible through relaxation and the awakening of powerful energies within you that you may experience sexual desires as well. All these types of desires need to be diverted as much as possible either though ignoring them or by acknowledging them and then allowing them to dissipate. Neither is an easy task I admit but, unlike itches or twitches, desires tend not to go away without some work on your part.

Common mental distractions include worry, skepticism, doubt, and stray thoughts. Entering the unknown territories in the deep recesses of the self can be a frightening thing. Doing so can cause you to worry or experience fear but if you do your work on becoming and remaining completely relaxed you should be able to ride this fear or other distracting feelings as you might ride a wave in the ocean. Skepticism and doubt often arise when you no longer are sure that what you are doing is achieving any results. This problem is related to the next two major distractions (goals and persistence) that we will discuss later in this section. By far the most common distraction is the appearance of stray unrelated thoughts. It is simply very difficult for the mind to remain still for any length of time. The purpose of the brain's existence, after all, is to process thoughts. When the mind is used to thinking at all times of the day and night and then suddenly it is asked to stop having any thoughts at all, it can become disoriented and even fearful. The mind can actually panic when it is not being used. At the point of panic the mind begins frantically scrambling to find any thought at all to process. As the meditator, it is your job to try and get the mind under control. Some have compared the process to breaking a wild horse. When you first get on top of the horse to try and control it, it begins to frantically buck and jump. It does not want to be under your control; it wants to run free. With persistence, however, you can stay on top of that horse until it finally gets exhausted and stops resisting. I am not suggesting that meditation requires that you stop all thoughts completely. This is one difficult method of meditation but it is not the only goal. What does need to happen is that your mind is put under your control. This can be done with several different methods of concentration. Mostly what you want to do is to have the mind stay focused on one particular thought or phrase and keep it on that track for as long as possible.

Emotional distractions can include disturbing feelings like anger or despair or you may experience a sudden lack of desire or will. Again, reaching into the depths of the self can be a daunting and frightening thing and there will often be internal resistance. You may dig up old feelings and remember past conflicts that your mind has buried for years. These things all need to be dragged out of the interior closet and brought out into the light. Old painful memories can be like little demons hiding in the basement. They live in the dark and damp places. You may have learned to ignore them or pretend that they are not there but they are there and they try to get noticed. They crave attention and they try to get it by annoying you or by creating obstacles in your life. They are the ones that make strange noises or flicker the lights on and off. Until you actually go down into that scary basement and pull those demons out they will continue to annoy you. You may come to experience the original pain and fear that led to the reason that they came to be there in the first place. Those feelings may arise mysteriously before you realize from where they originated. You might also lose your desire to continue to practice. This usually happens when you think that you are not getting out of the practice what you had hoped.

We often do not see the work of meditation as it grows through the dark places but eventually a leaf will emerge to the surface and a flower will grow.

Another possible reason for difficulty in your meditation practice is that your goals may be unclear. It helps to start out every session with a clear idea of what you hope to accomplish. You may have a grand goal in mind but you should realize that large goals may take time to accomplish. Small goals are easier to obtain so break down the great goal into smaller goals first. For example, you may take up meditation because you want to feel more at peace in your life. This may be a tall order for someone who might not feel this sense of peace on a regular basis. Try breaking up that goal into smaller goals. You might begin a session by saying that you want to experience a sense of deep peace for 10 minutes. The next time you may want to try and maintain a sense of peace for 20 minutes. Eventually, you can expand that same feeling into longer periods of time and into your daily life. It may also be possible that your goals are unrealistic for the practice you are doing. We have discussed some reasons that people use meditation but others often come up with unrealistic reasons. For some, the goal of meditating is to try and prove to themselves and to others that they are deeply spiritual people. People with such a goal will go through the motions of meditation but will not actually do any of the work needed to make it a meaningful spiritual practice. Clear goals are important because they make you think about exactly what you want to do and where you hope to go. They can also help you consider why you are taking on the practice in the first place. It helps to know why you are planning to take a particular journey and it helps to know where you plan to go. However, sometimes it is even best not to have any goal at all but to try, instead, to be open to the teachings and the experience of the meditation itself. I suggest that you take a moment now to consider your personal meditation goals and why you desire them. Write them down and keep them near your meditation space so that if you begin to get frustrated you may review your goals and your reasons. You might also find that your goals and reasons will change.

    Another reason for possible disappointment in your practice is that you may develop a lack of persistence. To achieve any results from meditation takes time. Some immediate results are possible but developing truly lasting long term effects is like planting a seed in the Spring. Though things are happening each and every time you meditate, it is not always so easy to see the results. At first they are small and imperceptible. The seed takes time to germinate under the ground. After several sessions you may experience a small breakthrough as when the seedling breaks through the ground. With more time, attention, and care, the work you planted will eventually flower. Buddhists use the image of the lotus flower to represent awakening through meditation. The lotus flower grows in swamps. Its seed is planted at the bottom of a muddy pond and germinates unseen in the dark waters. As it grows, it works its way up through the murky waters. Eventually, a green leaf grows on the surface of the water and a beautiful lotus flower emerges from the leaf. We often do not see the work of meditation as it grows through the dark places but eventually a leaf will emerge to the surface and a flower will grow. Without the patience to see this process through, the flower will never have a chance to work its way to the surface. Unfortunately, our society teaches that we can have whatever we want right away. There is the quick meal, the drive-thru, and the disposable razor, for example. The person whose lifestyle accepts this message has a difficult time being patient with the slowly evolving process of development that takes place through meditation. The only remedy for this impatience is a faith in the process and persistence in seeing it through. Once you find a procedure that works for you, stick with it for some time and allow it to slowly work before trying another. Sometimes it is necessary to try a different method or focus but often it is best to give one method a chance first. How do you know when it is time to try something new? That is a hard question to answer because there is no single way to determine the best answer. Try and get something out of each exercise and method that you develop before changing. No matter how you meditate, if you are honestly giving a chosen method a chance to work, something will eventually happen. It may be a small development but there is something to be gained from nearly every effort. Mostly, listen to your body – deep down inside. It knows when something is right.

Another negative message that often develops from our society is that failure is a bad thing and should be avoided at all costs. This is simply not true. Failure is part of the process of growing. All growing involves pain and effort and failing to achieve something the first time is part of the process of learning how to make a better attempt. Failure is not a reason for shame. Because a person fails to succeed in one task does not make him or her a failure in life. Accept failure as part of the process of meditation. Just as Dabrowski's levels of emotional development and Underhill's stage of the Dark Night of the Soul illustrate, encountering disappointment and working your way through that disappointment can be part of a healthy growth cycle.

Sometimes what you perceive to be a failure is actually a success. You may not have achieved the goal for which you set out but you may have come across exactly what you needed to find. In the process of meditation you may come across some emotional, mental, or spiritual barriers that you did not know existed. Encountering them may feel like failure but may only be a temporary roadblock or a necessary challenge of the path on which you need to proceed. As you develop and continue to practice, be open and flexible about your goals and be ready to accept whatever may come your way. Try not to judge yourself too harshly about your expectations. Let each perceived failure become a lesson for you and a reason to strengthen your resolve.

Preparing to Meditate – the Four Ps

Before you begin to meditate your should take some time to prepare so that your experience and practice will be the best that it can be. To help remember how to best prepare I use what I call the four "P"s which are: *Person, Place, Posture,* and *Persistence.* The first "P", Person, concerns preparation of the self. It might just as easily have been called purification because that is what you will seek to do – purify yourself so that you are ready to begin meditating. Once again, I will refer to the four parts of the self in purifying the self.

To purify the body it is good to have a clean body that is supple and ready to begin. Stretching is a good way to get the body ready for meditating. It promotes relaxation and the act of stretching itself helps promote deep breathing and lets you prepare yourself for meditative practice. There are exercises at the end of this chapter which include some suggestions for stretching and breathing. Sometimes it helps to put on special clothing for meditation. Things like robes or ritual wear can help signal to your body that it is time to meditate. Your meditation practice should be something special that you do for yourself. Having a special item of clothing to wear when you practice helps to set that practice apart from the other mundane activities of your day. To purify your mind, try to let it also relax. Let go of the daily worries and concerns. Clear your mind out. Also, be sure to clear away and prevent any mental distractions during your meditation time. Turn off any phones or alarms you might have. Consider any other noises or activities that may be in your space which may distract your attention and then see to it that they are disabled. Ask others in your household or meditation space to not disturb you while you are practicing.

Purification of the heart involves allowing your heart to be open and compassionate. Harboring anger and holding grudges only weighs down the heart and makes it difficult to receive new feelings. That is not to say that there is not a place for anger and frustration because such emotions may cause you to act when action is necessary but during meditation these types of feelings are not only unnecessary, they make it difficult to proceed. To the best of your ability and practice, the heart needs to be just as open and relaxed as your body. This is not a state of no-feeling. When the heart is open and ready to receive, it is in a state of compassion. The word compassion is defined in dictionaries as a sense of awareness of the suffering of others but I believe it is more than that. For me, to be "com-passionate" means to be open to sharing all conditions of the self and others. In effect, you are being passionate in conjunction with others. You are open and able to experience all the sufferings as well as all the joys of yourself and others. To be compassionate under this definition is truly challenging because it requires you to be open to all levels of relationships: yourself, others, the world, and Spirit.

You can be open to experiencing your own energy, the energy of others, the energy of all beings and the energy of Spirit.

Purification of the soul is similar to the idea of purification of the heart except that the focus is on connection. An open soul is free to make connections between the self, others, the world, and Spirit. It is like connecting a wire to another power source and allowing the electricity to flow freely along the wire. You can be open to experiencing your own energy, the energy of others, the energy of all beings and the energy of Spirit. Be ready to accept and share in these energies as you begin to experience them in your practice.

The second "P," Place, reminds you to make a special space for your meditation. You can prepare a small corner of one room or an entire room and claim it as a meditation space. Having such a space can be beneficial to your practice. When you come to a place that is specially designated for meditation it helps signal to you that it is time to begin your practice. Also, all the things you need for your practice will already be there and you will be ready to begin right away. A meditation space needs to be big enough to allow room for you to assume your posture and to hold any materials you wish to use. At the very least the space should include a pillow or mat for you to sit or lay upon, some room or a table to place objects upon, and possibly some storage space to hold special tools and items you may need. An ideal place is somewhere where you can construct a small altar and have room in front of it to meditate. There you could place a special chair, pillow, or mat for your practice. With an altar, you can make meditation part of a complete ritual practice, if you so desire. Once you have chosen a place, make it sacred. Clear and cleanse the space in your own way and make it special so that when you enter that space you will know it is time to enter into a new internal space as well.

Posture is the third "P." Give some thought on how you want your body to be situated when meditating. The classic image is of someone sitting in a full lotus position on the floor. This particular posture is not a required form for meditating and may even be disadvantageous to your particular body. Yogis and other long time meditators stretch for hours and hours in order to get their legs to assume those difficult postures. Your body may simply not be ready or even designed to sit in the same way. Some people sit during meditation and some people do not. You can lie down and meditate but it is generally not recommended since it can encourage sleep while sitting helps you maintain some awareness. If you find that sitting for long periods of time is difficult for you and distracts you from your work then, by all means, try a lying position but you may need to maintain an extra strong focus so that you do not drift off to sleep. Any sitting position that encourages a straight but not stiff back and which allows you to be even and balanced with the floor can be an effective position. Using a chair is also possible although an overly comfortable chair may also cause you to sleep. A chair with a soft bottom and some back and side support might be sufficient. The key is to find a position that is comfortable to you but not so comfortable that you cannot maintain a state of awareness. When your entire body is supported as it is lying down or in a plush armchair it naturally wants to drift off to sleep. I prefer to sit on a big cushion in a half lotus (one leg over the other) position but you should take some time to experiment on your own to find out what works for you. Also keep in mind that you do not have to be stiff or unmoving in that position. Once you begin your work you should try to remain still and relaxed as much as possible but remember that this is not meditative boot camp! If you feel a cramp coming on or the blood in your legs is being cut off, then change your position. If you can do it slowly and without breaking your concentration it will not diminish your practice. The point is not to be stiff but to be solid enough that you do not slink away as you practice. Many people begin their practice with their eyes closed though some keep their eyes open to focus on a particular object. Once again, you will need to decide which is more comfortable to you. Here is a list of some possible postures that can be used for meditation.

Meditation Sitting Positions

1. Lying down.
2. Sitting with legs crossed.
3. Half Lotus sitting (one foot rests on the knee of the other leg).
4. Full Lotus sitting (both feet rest on the knees).
5. Japanese sitting (both legs are folded under so that the buttocks rest on the soles).
6. Chair sitting.

Illustration 13: Meditation Positions

The final "P" in the set is Persistence. This is the most challenging part of preparing to meditate. You have established that you are ready, you have a place to meditate, you have found a position that is comfortable, and you have determined a schedule for your practice. Now you just need to commit yourself to doing it. Meditation takes persistence in practice in order to achieve any results. I suggest that you give yourself at least 6 months to a year of practice before you decide whether or not meditation is for you. During that time, commit yourself to a regular practice and persist in it even if you do not think anything is happening. Changes as a result of meditative practice are often very subtle. Some people practice for years before they begin to notice a change but almost everyone I know who has regularly practiced meditation has noticed some type of change over time. It is best if you can designate a regular time for your practice. Choose whether you can and want to meditate once a week, several times a week, or every day and then create a schedule that allows you to do that. I prefer the early morning hours before work when everything is quiet and the fresh energy of a new day begins to fill the house. Choose a regular time and day and stick with it. Let meditation become part of your routine so that you get used to doing it regularly.

Developing a Meditation Procedure

You can make meditation as simple or as complex as you want. You can, for example, simply sit in a cross-legged position at any time or any place you choose whenever you feel like you need a few moments of internal peace. You can sit for just a few moments and then get up and go. If meditation is this simple for you then you may want to skip this particular section but if it takes more effort for you to switch your mind from processing the never ending range of information and emotions that fill most of our days to a frame of mind that is more quiet and focused, then you may want to consider developing a specific procedure for your meditation practice. Just as in a ritual, the meditation procedure helps guide your body, mind, heart, and soul into a state of meditation. It is a way of transporting yourself from the mundane world to a special place of your own where you can feel free to meditate. Setting up a meditation routine may, at first, seem to be like an unwieldy addition to your meditative goals but it is worth the time and effort. When you first create a procedure it is a bit daunting but it is like learning to ride a bike or drive a car. A meditation procedure is a short practice you can do to enter into a meditative state. Once you have developed and practiced a procedure then it will go from being a set of individual chores to being an easy flowing process that will signal to you that it is time to move into meditation. I encourage you to develop a procedure that works for you but I will present one here that you can begin to work on your own.

The process I have designed for the Outer Procedure is built in a similar way that I approach ritual work. There are a total of 13 steps. The first six are designed to bring you into a meditative state from which you can then do your Inner Procedure which prepares you to do your main meditation focus. Step seven is where that particular work would occur. Steps 8 – 13 bring you out of the meditation and return you to where you began. Imagine a swirl of energy that spirals down like a tornado. When you first begin to enter into meditation your thoughts are scattered and unfocused just like the outer swirls of the tornado. You begin on the outside of the spiral. As you work through the procedure you begin to center in and focus your thoughts and energies. It is like entering into the spiral until the swirls of energy get smaller and more focused. By step seven you have become focused and are prepared to begin the inner procedure and then your main focus. After your meditation work is complete you then unwind that spiral and work your way out again.

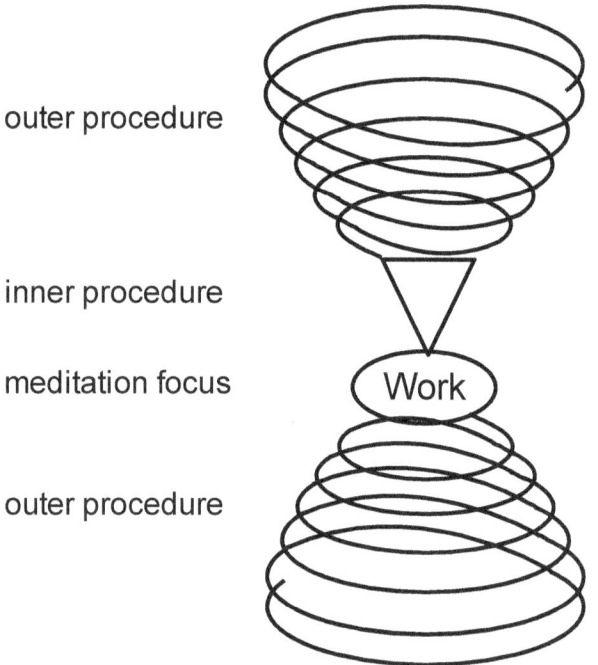

Illustration 14: The Inner and Outer Procedures

> **Outer Meditation Procedure Steps**
>
> 1. Stretch
> 2. Center
> 3. Connect
> 4. Enter In
> 5. Invocation
> 6. Intention
> 7. The Work
> 8. Acknowledgment
> 9. Release
> 10. Exit
> 11. Disconnect
> 12. Collect
> 13. Stretch

Illustration 15: Outer Procedure Steps

Begin your meditation session with a short but effective set of stretches. Stretching helps to wake the body and prepare it to sit for an extended period of time. It helps improve circulation and posture and aids in the process of relaxing by relieving muscle tension. When stretching, remember to always balance your movements. If you do a stretch on one side of your body do the same stretch on the other side as well. To stretch properly, move your body in such a way that you can begin to feel the tension in the muscle. Do not over stretch or bounce the stretch because damage can occur to the muscles and remember to breathe fully as you go. Stretching should be done to all the major areas of the body: the neck, the arms (including the shoulders, forearms, biceps, and triceps) the stomach, the back, and the legs (including the calf, hip, thighs, and hamstrings). Stretching can also be an activity in which you learn to access and move internal energies. By focusing on the breath while moving into stretching positions you can experience the movement of internal energies and learn to increase and strengthen the flow of energy in the body. Doing so can help maintain good health in body, mind, heart, and soul. Practices such as Yoga and Gi Gung can be used for creating a stretching and energy movement routine as well. The end of this chapter has several exercises to help you explore ways in which you can create your procedures.

To center means to align your body with the floor and your meditation space. Connecting means to relate to that space through a visualization that helps connect you to your environment. I use the term "enter in" to represent the process of going into an inner space to begin meditation. I have taught students to create what I call the Inner Temple through a personal visualization. The Inner Temple is a place you create in your mind which is purely your own. It is a very personal space that helps you to set the stage for entering into the spiritual work of meditation. From your temple you can connect to whatever energies or deities you may call. However, the space does not necessarily need to be a temple; it can be whatever you want it to be. After centering and connecting, you should then focus on your breathing. Concentrating on the breath can be a powerful meditation on its own. Slow down your breath until you feel as if your entire body is breathing fully and slowly. Follow your breath as it moves in and out of your body and feel the sensation of relaxation that it gives to you before moving on to the next step.

While in the inner space you can then invoke your deity or whatever energy of the ultimate reality to which you wish to connect. Doing so helps you to bring into your space that energy you wish to incorporate into your practice. Even if you do not wish to consider an invocation to a deity or energy source you can, at the least, use the time to recognize that you are a part of a larger reality. As you meditate, you may come into contact with realities beyond your own. Accepting that early on in your practice will allow you to more easily make those connections. You may not even know what it is you are touching and whether or not it is within you or something from far beyond (though it is actually both). Do not be in a hurry to understand everything that may happen during your meditations. Allow yourself to enter into the mystery. If you do wish to recognize a deity or energy source then you may find that you can draw upon that ultimate mystery as a source for your work. During this time of invocation you may offer a prayer or blessing for your work. Before invoking any energy, however, I do suggest that you create an inner circle in your inner temple. Make a magic circle that will offer you protection. As you create a circle you may also wish to call upon the four directions and the two layers (Above and Below) to complete your magickal space.

The next step is to focus on stating the intention of your meditation session. You may do this internally and silently. By clearly stating an intention, you make clear in your mind what it is that you hope to do during your meditation time. This clarity helps you to focus on your goal and not waste time trying to decide what it is you want to do. More than just announcing your goals, however, stating your intention also sends that intent into the sacred space you have created and sends it toward whatever power, energy, or deity you may have invoked in the previous step.

After you have completed these steps then you will have entered into your meditative space and will be ready for the inner procedure. The inner procedure is yet another means of engaging your whole self into a deeper state of preparation. After the inner procedure you will be ready to begin the actual work you have decided to do. At this point you might want to turn on a musical recording or a recording that guides you through a specific meditation. You will begin your focus on the goal or object you have chosen before you began your procedure or you may choose to do an unfocused meditation.

After the main meditation work is completed, it is time to begin the process of coming back to the world by coming out of the spiral. The first step

Sometimes lessons take time to reveal their wisdom to us.

in that process is called acknowledgment. In this step you can take just a brief moment to thank whatever powers, deities, or energies you may have called upon in your invocation or that you may have encountered during your meditation. Thank them for teaching and guiding you on your way even if you are not sure what you have learned. You might consider offering a prayer or blessing. Sometimes lessons take time to reveal their wisdom to us. Taking this action reminds us that we are not the sole teacher and guide for our learning. If you have connected to something in your meditation then it is only right to thank the universe or whomever you may have reached for what you have learned and experienced. Even if nothing was learned (seemingly) then it is still good to thank the universe for giving you a chance to experience its peacefulness even if for but a brief time. After thanking any deities or energies, it is time to let them go their way. In this step, ask all that you may have invoked earlier to go on their way. If you created an inner circle, called upon the four directions, or called upon the two layers, then release them in the opposite order that you called them in.

Next, exit your inner temple or sacred place in the opposite way that you entered it. Allow yourself some time to travel from that place back to where you are now. When you have returned, disconnect yourself from the earth and sky so that you will again be free to move. If you used the tree image then pull in your roots and branches slowly and carefully. Remember that though you are disconnecting, your energies will never be completely disconnected from the earth and sky. You will always be a part of both but will not be bound to one particular place.

I call the next step collecting yourself. In this step I suggest that you just sit quietly for a few moments before you get up to leave your meditation space. Enjoy the sensation of a relaxed body, a still mind, an open heart, and a connected soul. To experience this sort of peace and joy even if for a brief time is truly a gift from the universe. Allow yourself to enjoy it. Afterwards, rise slowly from your space and do a very brief final stretch to allow the muscles that have not been moved during your meditation time to unwind.

I realize that all this may seem overly complex for someone who might just want to take a few moments to meditate every day but I assure you that the effort is worth it. Developing these skills separately will take some time but the actual goal of this text is to help you develop a series of very short procedures before and after your meditation and to provide suggestions for the actual meditative focus. When you have finished all the exercises in the book you should be able to develop a very short Outer and Inner procedure (each one or two minutes in length) and then be able to move into a deep meditative practice. The Outer Procedure at the end of your practice will also be a short procedure for helping you to return.

Chapter Two

Summary

Meditation can be as simple or as complex as you want to make it. If it is relatively easy for you to just sit, block out the distractions of the world, and focus your mind for an extended period of time, then you need only to determine when and on what you plan to meditate and you may be able to skip the first few chapters of this book. The rest will come naturally. If, however, all these things do not come so easy to you then it may be beneficial for you to work on developing the separate skills you need to enter into meditation effectively by reading all the chapters in this book. There are many reasons why someone may not be able to meditate successfully but most of these pitfalls can be avoided through careful preparation, by setting up a meditation routine, and by committing yourself to a regular practice without seeking immediate results. I suggest that this regular routine include an Outer and Inner procedure that you do each time you begin and end your meditation practice. Such a routine will need to be done consciously by practicing individual parts separately but those will all be brought together to create brief unified procedures that will alert your body, mind, heart, and soul to the fact that you are about to enter into a meditative state. At the end of your procedures you will be ready to begin the specific meditative work that you have chosen to do and the Outer Procedure done in a reverse order will signal to you that it is time to return to the everyday world. In the next section I will offer several exercises designed to help you develop each of the separate parts of an Outer Procedure and then I will show you how to put them all together.

Exercises

Each of the following exercises are meant to be done as separate practices. In effect, they are each individual meditations that are designed to help you devise a complete procedure but each one can be done as a practice on its own. Approach each one as a unique exercise first. You may find that you have to do some only once but others may need to be repeated to get the full effect of each one. After completing each exercise, determine for yourself if you are ready to move on to the next. After all the exercises have been completed then the final exercise will show how to put them all together. Though each one will take some time and practice, the final procedure you eventually develop should only take a few moments to complete.

Part One - Stretching

I have included four types of stretching and moving exercises in this section so that you may find one that best suits your needs and inclinations. I will introduce a short stretch, a longer stretch, a short form of Tai Chi that I have adopted as a Pagan form and a version of the Yoga Sun Salutation that some Pagans will find useful as a stretch and a tribute to the sun and the morning. Of course, you can devise your own by combining any of the ideas presented. What is important is that you find a way to gently stretch all the major muscle areas of your body with a special emphasis on the legs if you plan to do a sitting meditation for a long time. Remember to do each stretch slowly and evenly. Move into the stretch until you just begin to feel resistance and hold that position until the muscles begin to release their tension then move back or stretch a little bit further if you wish to continue. Never bounce or force a stretch. As you hold the position, remember to breathe evenly and fully. Try not to hold your breath. I will discuss moving energy in each of these stretches as well for those who wish to add this dimension to their stretches.

Exercise 2.1 – Basic stretch

The following exercise will help you develop a simple stretching routine to help you prepare your body to meditate for a long time.

Chapter Two

Exercise no.	6 (2.1)
Goal	To stretch the body
Minimum length of time	5 minutes
Location	anywhere
Needs	none
Steps	

1. *Reach Up.* To begin this basic routine stand with your feet together (about shoulder width) with your arms at your side. Bring your arms up over your head and reach up while looking up. Feel the stretch in your back and front as well as in your arms and neck. Lift your head so that you feel the stretch along your spine and into your neck. Pull your arms and feel the stretch throughout them. Spread your fingers and turn your palms up so that you feel the stretch in your hands and fingers.
2. *Bend Down.* Next, bend down slowly until you feel the stretch in your back and legs. Go only as far as you can until you just begin to feel the stretch. If you can bend all the way down and touch the floor, great, but do not attempt to do so if it is not comfortable. Try to bend as far as you can with your legs straight. Keep the knees straight but do not lock the knees. If this is difficult for you then bend the knees slightly as you bend down. When you are done return to your standing position.
3. *Reach Forward.* Turn your palms outward and bend forward to about a 90 degree angle. Let your head point down. Stretch your back, shoulders, and neck. When you are done let your hands return to your side and return to your standing position.
4. *Reach Right.* Bring your left hand up over your head. Bend your body to your right with your left hand pointing to the right over your head and your right hand at your side with fingers pointing down. Feel the stretch in your left side and neck. Return to your standing position.
5. *Reach Back.* Bring both hands up above your head. Bend back slightly until you feel a stretch in your stomach and your upper back. Point your fingers to the space behind you and let your head lift up. Do not drop your head back since this is not a good position for your head. Instead look straight up and feel the stretch in your neck and shoulders. Return to your standing position.

6. *Reach Left.* Bring your right hand over your head then bend to the left in the same way that you bent to the right. Return to your standing position.
7. *Lift Knee – Right.* To stretch your legs begin by lifting your knee to your chest as best you can. If you can do this while balancing on your left foot then all the better but some will need to steady themselves by holding onto the back of a chair or some other method of support. An even more effective stretch can be done by lifting the right foot up toward the left side of your waist while lifting the knee as high as possible. Feel the stretch in your buttocks and upper leg. When you are done return your knee forward.
8. *Leg Back – Right.* Grasp your ankle and gently pull it up from behind you. You should feel the stretch in your thighs. When you are done let your foot come down until you are again in your standing position.
9. *Step Left.* Point your left foot to the left and take a large step to the left. Keep your right foot planted where it is and bend your left knee. Keep moving slowly to the left until you feel the stretch in your groin area. This stretch is especially important for allowing blood to flow into your legs while sitting for a long period of time so give yourself some time to let this stretch be effective. When you are done come back to your standing position.
10. *Lift Knee – Left.* Lift your left knee up just as you did your right knee and stretch the buttocks then bring the knee forward.
11. *Leg Back – Left.* Bring your left foot up behind you until you feel the stretch in your thigh then return to your standing position.
12. *Step Right.* Point your right foot to the right then step to the right keeping your left foot in place. Bend your right knee and move until you feel a stretch in your groin. Return to your standing position.
13. *Sit.* If you use a meditation cushion you may want to put it just behind you at this point. Bend over slowly to give a second stretch to your back and legs then bend your knees until your hands can touch the floor. Crawl forward with your hands until you can put your legs into your sitting position then bring yourself up into that sitting position. You should now be sitting in your space or on your cushion and ready to take the next step in your meditation practice.

Exercise 2.2 – The Basic Stretch With Breathing

Chapter Two

    Practice these steps several times and work to put them together into a seamless flowing routine. After you have done that it is time to add the breath to each movement. By adding the breath to the routine, you create a type of meditation out of the stretching routine itself. In general, every time you move away from the standing position breathe out and every time you return, breathe in. Try to imagine breathing with your whole body and not just your lungs. Visualize your whole body filling with air and then gently releasing that air. Every time you exhale, feel your body releasing tension. The same routine with the movement of the breath added might look like the following.

Just Being

Exercise no.	7 (2.1)
Goal	Stretching with breathing
Minimum length of time	5 minutes
Location	anywhere
Needs	none
Steps	

1. Reach Up.
    a) Inhale as you bring your arms up.
    b) Exhale as you keep your arms up.
2. Bend Down.
    a) Inhale before you begin.
    b) Exhale as you bend down.
3. Reach Forward.
    a) Inhale as you come up.
    b) Exhale as you reach forward.
4. Reach Right.
    a) Inhale as you return to the standing position.
    b) Exhale as you reach right.
5. Reach Back.
    a) Inhale as you return to the standing position.
    b) Exhale as you reach back.
6. Reach Left.
    a) Inhale as you return to the standing position.
    b) Exhale as you reach left.
7. Lift Knee – Right.
    a) Inhale as you return to the standing position.
    b) Exhale as you lift the knee.
8. Leg Back – Right.
    a) Inhale as you bring your knee forward.
    b) Exhale as you bring your foot back.
9. Step Left.
    a) Inhale as you return to the standing position.
    b) Exhale as you step left.
10. Lift Knee – Left.
    a) Inhale as you return.
    b) Exhale as you lift the knee.
11. *Leg Back – Left.*
    a) Inhale as you bring your knee forward.
    b) Exhale as you bring your foot back.
12. *Step Right.*
    a) Inhale as you return.

Chapter Two

> b) Exhale as you step right.
> 13. *Sit.*
>   a) Inhale as you return.
>   b) Exhale as you bend over.
>   c) Inhale, then exhale as you move forward.
>   d) Inhale, then exhale as you sit.

Another dimension may be added to the stretching routine by considering the movement of energy which is connected to the movement of the breath. If you have never done anything like this before then try this preliminary exercise: sit in a comfortable position and relax. Allow yourself to breath fully and slowly. As you breathe in imagine energy entering your body through the pores of your skin and as you breathe out let that energy fill your body and return. When you have got the hang of this technique then apply it to your stretching routine with the breathing added. Every time you breathe into a move, feel the energy come into your body and every time you breathe out to a new position feel that energy move through your body and return.

You might note that the first six steps of this stretching routine touch all parts of a magickal sphere that you can create around you. The first two can be used to connect to the directions of Above and Below (what I call the Layers) while steps 3 – 6 connect you to each of the four directions. In this way you can connect your breath and the movement of energy to create a sacred circle around you before you begin your meditation practice. Try doing Exercise 7 while moving energy within your body.

You can, of course, add or subtract to the list of stretches above to make your routine longer or shorter. It is a basic routine designed to stretch most of the large muscle groups but it does not stretch every muscle in the body. If you want to add to the routine consider including stretches for the muscles in the arms, the neck, the hip, and the muscles in the feet, just to name a few.

Exercise 2.3 – Sitting Stretch

An even shorter stretch can be done while sitting which makes a good quick warm-up for a sitting meditation. Just like the longer one above, this stretch is designed to create a sphere around your meditation space. Steps 1 and 2 connect you with the Layers while steps 4 -7 connect you with the four directions. Step 10 allows you to fill your space with energy and connect to Center. Begin by sitting on the floor or a cushion with your legs in front of you. This exercise assumes you are facing North but can be done in any direction.

Chapter Two

Exercise no.	8 (2.3)
Goal	Creating a sitting stretching routine
Minimum length of time	5 minutes
Location	anywhere
Needs	none
Steps	

1. *Fill Your Space.* Breathe in and raise your arms above you from your center. As you bring up your arms draw in energy into your whole body as you move. Breathe out and let your arms come down in an arc. Let the energy you have drawn in fill your space.
2. *Reach Up.* Breathe in. Bring your hands above you and reach up as far as you can stretch. Extend the energy just above you.
3. *Bend Forward.* Breathe out. With your legs extended forward lean forward until you feel a stretch in your back and legs, then return. Try to point your hands and head downward. Breathe in as you come back up. Extend your energy to just below you.
4. *Butterfly.* Breathe out. Bring the heels of your feet in toward your center and let your knees point away from you. Bring your feet in as close as possible and let your knees go down. Lean forward slightly until you feel the stretch in your groin. When you are done, breathe in and cross your legs in whatever way is most comfortable for you. Feel the energy in your center.
5. *Lean Forward.* Breathe out. Point your hands forward and lean forward slightly keeping your head looking forward. Extend the energy to the North. Breathe in as you return to your sitting position.
6. *Lean Right.* Breathe out. Place your right hand beside you on the floor. Bring your left hand over your head pointing the fingers to the right and lean right until you feel a stretch in your left side. Return to your sitting position. Extend the energy to the East. Breathe in as you return.
7. *Lean Back.* Breathe out. Place both hands behind you and lean back. Extend the energy to the South. Breathe in as you return.
8. *Lean Left.* Breathe out. Place your left hand beside you on the floor. Bring your right hand over your head pointing the fingers to the left and lean left until you feel a stretch in your

> right side. Extend the energy to the West. Breathe in as you return.
> 9. *Side Twist – Right*. Breathe out. Place your hands on your hips. Twist your body to the right until your right elbow is pointing behind you. Look behind you as best as you can until you feel a stretch in your back. Breathe in as you return.
> 10. *Side Twist – Left*. Breathe out. Do the same thing as above but in the opposite direction. Breathe in as you return. Breathe out as you let your hands go out to the side and down.

Exercise 2.4 – Pagan Tai Chi

Tai Chi is an excellent Taoist method of stretching, moving, and experiencing the flow of energy called Chi. There are many patterns of movements or forms that can be quite long and require a good deal of open space. I have adopted a few of the movements here to create a short movement pattern that helps create a sacred space and bring energy into that space for use in meditation. I call it Pagan Tai Chi.

Before beginning the movement, however, I need to mention a few basic principles of Tai Chi that will apply to my short form as well. There are three basic stances that should be mastered before learning a routine. They are the Standing Stance, the Open Stance, and the Warrior Stance. Different schools will have different names for each of these but they are all basic to Tai Chi. The Standing Stance (or Beginning Stance) involves simply standing with your feet just slightly apart (about shoulder width). The feet are slightly angled and the arms are left down comfortably at your side. The body should be straight but not stiff. The posture should be something between a military stance and a slight slouch. In this stance you should be able to relax but also be ready to move. One basic principle of Tai Chi is called *Sinking In*. In the Open Stance (or Riding Horse Stance) the knees are slightly bent and the hands are turned slightly forward. You should feel as if your weight is sinking in to the center of your body (just below your navel). Imagine that you are holding a large and heavy ball about the size of one of those work-out balls. In the Warrior Stance (Bow and Arrow Stance) your legs form an "L" shape.

To form this stance, place your ankles together at a 90° angle one pointing forward and the other pointing to the side. Now move the side pointing foot straight until it reaches just beyond the shoulder. Shift your weight until it is evenly distributed in the middle between your two legs. Bend your knees and sink in. This is a very strong position and, if done right, makes it very hard for anyone to push you over. I often use it when I am on a crowded subway and cannot grab on to a handle.

    The particular Tai Chi form I have created has several purposes. For one, I wanted a form that could be done in a relatively small space. Many long Tai Chi forms require much space to move. As with the stretching routine above, I wanted a form that could create a sacred space in preparation for meditation. This form emphasizes the flow of energy from Earth through the body and is used to create a magickal space by moving that energy to the directions of Above and Below as well as the four cardinal directions and Center. The form is divided into three parts. The first creates a capsule shaped bubble of energy stretching from above and below (the Layers.) Part two uses a short set of movements which are done the same way four times to honor and extend energies to the four directions - the bubble of energy gets shaped into a sphere. (Some prefer to think of the surrounding space as an egg shaped form.) Part three focuses on ending the set by bringing energy to the Center.

Exercise no.	9a (2.4)
Goal	To practice a Pagan form of Tai Chi for stretching
Minimum length of time	1 minute
Location	anywhere
Needs	none
Steps	(Part 1 - Setting The Layers)

1. Setting the Layers
    1.1. *Beginning.* Begin in the open stance facing North. Breathe in and bring both arms up in front of you with fingers pointing down. Breathe out, let your hands flip up with fingers pointing up and bring your arms slowly down to your side where you began.
    1.2. *Hold the ball.* Breathe in bringing your hands forward and up to the sides. As you breathe in, draw in energy into your body. Breathe out and form a large ball in front of you with your arms. Focus energy into this ball.
    1.3. *Reach Up.* Breathe in and raise the ball of energy above your head. As you move your arms, send the energy of the ball up above your head like a protective canopy. Breathe out and let your arms arc out and downwards in a circle and bring them round until they are in front of you at your waist - fingers touching – as if holding another ball.
    1.4. *Push down.* Breathe in. Bring your hands and arms (still bent at the elbows as if holding a ball) up in front of you as if moving to the top of the ball. Your hands should end up at the height of your chin with palms facing down. Breathe out. Push your hands downward to the floor while bending over. Send the energy down below your feet to create a capsule shaped bubble of energy above and below you. Come slowly back up and let your hands come to your sides.

Chapter Two

Exercise no.	9b (2.4)
Goal	Pagan Tai Chi
Minimum length of time	1 minute
Location	anywhere
Needs	none
Steps	(Part 2 – Setting the Four Directions)

2. Setting the Four Directions.
    2.1. Setting the North.
    a) *Ward Off Left.* Breathe in. Bring your left hand up to your right shoulder palm facing out. Put your weight on your right foot. Sink in. Breathe out. Sweep your left hand across and in front of you (as if warding off a punch in slow motion) then let it drop down to your left side. Put your weight to your left and even it out to create an open stance.
    b) *Ward off right and form a ball.* Breathe in. Bring your right hand up to your left shoulder palm facing out. Put your weight on your left foot. Turn your right foot to the right 90°. Breathe out. Shift your weight to create the horse stance. Let your right hand come down to your hip in front of you palm up. Bring your left hand up and over to your chin palm facing down to form another ball. You should now be facing East. Send energy into the ball as you did in the first part.
    c) *Compress the ball.* Breathe in. Shift your weight to your right foot. Bring your left foot in until it touches your right ankle toes touching the ground. Breathe out. Move your left foot forward (North) and create the horse stance facing North. Bring your right hand back and turn it so the fingers are pointing up palm facing North. The left hand will curve forward until it is just about shoulder height and about a foot in front of your right shoulder. The right hand will push forward until it meets your left. Concentrate on compressing the ball of energy until it is about the size of a golf ball in your hands. You should now be facing North with your hands holding the compressed ball of energy.
    d) *Pushing Forward.* Breathe in while you separate your hands. Your right hand will drop down while your

left hand will rise up. Shift your weight to your right foot and bring your left foot back towards your right ankle toes touching the floor. Breathe out. Curve your left hand in a big arc over your head and then turn it palm out. Do the opposite with your right hand. Turn it over in a downward arc then bring the palm facing forward. Breathe out while you shift your weight back to the left foot moving it forward to once again create the horse stance facing North. As you step forward push both hands forward. The right hand will have fingers pointing upwards while the left hand sill have fingers pointing to the right to for a kind of "T." Push the energy of the ball forward to the North.

e) *Turn.* Breathe in as you continue to shift your weight to the left foot allowing you to turn your right foot to the right 45°. Breathe out as you shift your weight to the right. Let both hands drop down to your sides while you bring your left foot in. Even out your weight. You should now be facing East in a standing position.

f) *Bow.* Breathe in and bring your hands out in a large circular motion to your sides until they come together over your head. Breathe out and bring your hands down together in front of you. Bow in recognition to the direction of East then let your arms return to your sides.

2.2. *Setting the East.* Follow the same directions for 2.1 to 2.6 but in the direction of the East. You should end up facing South.

2.3. *Setting the South.* Follow the same directions for 2.1 to 2.6 but in the direction of the South. You should end up facing West.

2.4. *Setting the West.* Follow the same directions for 2.1 to 2.6 but in the direction of the West. You should end up facing North.

Exercise 2.5 The Sun Salutation

This routine is taken from the tradition of Yoga. It is meant to be a complete stretching routine and is believed to have been used by Yogis in the early mornings to greet the sun.

Chapter Two

Exercise no.	10 (2.5)
Goal	A stretching routine
Minimum length of time	1 minute
Location	preferable outdoors at dawn
Needs	none
Steps	

1. Stand with the hands in front of you in a prayer position. Exhale.
2. Inhale as you bring your arms up and back. Bend back and stretch. Look behind you.
3. Exhale as you bend over and place your hands just outside of your feet. Bend your knees if you need to.
4. Inhale as you bring the right foot back and place the right knee on the floor. Look upwards.
5. Hold the breath as you bring the left foot back and hold your shoulders off the floor. Look down.
6. Exhale as you lower your shoulders to the floor.
7. Inhale as let your body rest on the floor and you push your shoulders up off the floor. Look up.
8. Exhale as you lift your buttocks off the floor and bring your feet in until you have created an inverted "V" shape with your body. Look down.
9. Inhale as you step forward with your left foot until it is next to your left hand. Look up.
10. Exhale as you bring your right foot to your right hand and lift your buttocks until you are bent over just as in position 3.
11. Inhale as you bring your arms up and back and bend backwards. Look behind you.
12. Exhale as you gently return to a standing position with your arms at your side.

Part Two - Centering and Collecting

The purpose of centering is to literally center yourself with the floor of the space you are in and with Earth. As you first practice this technique it will take a conscious effort but the technique will eventually become easy and quick. This exercise will end with what I call *collecting* where you sit quietly for just a few moments and collect your thoughts while you also enjoy the quiet and peacefulness of the moment.

Exercise 2.6 – Centering With The Floor

This exercise will help you center yourself with the space around you so that you can be comfortable and feel connected.

Exercise no.	11 (2.6)
Goal	Center the body
Minimum length of time	15 seconds
Location	anywhere
Needs	none
Steps	

1. Get into your sitting position.
2. Feel your legs or feet against the floor (depending upon your position).
3. Rock your legs and feet back and forth until you feel that they are evenly balanced with the floor.
4. Rock yourself gently from side to side until your upper body feels evenly balanced then do the same by rocking gently from front to back.
5. Softly roll your shoulders until they become balanced.
6. Depending on the position of your hands and arms find a way to roll them gently from one side to the other until they feel evenly balanced with Earth.
7. Gently roll your head until you can find a balanced midway point between side to side and front to back positions. Your whole body now should feel evenly balanced with the floor and with Earth.
8. While in this balanced position take a few moments to enjoy the feeling of being at rest with Earth.
9. Collect your thoughts by focusing on the sensation of your body. Allow this moment of quiet joy to be a special gift to yourself.

Exercise 2.7 – Adding the Breath

You can also add the breath to this practice by breathing in while you roll your body and then letting out the breath when you have centered. Do this exercise while working on centering your body.

Exercise no.	12 (2.7)
Goal	Adding the breath while centering
Minimum length of time	30 seconds
Location	anywhere
Needs	none
Steps	

1. Breathe in slowly and fully as you rock your chest from side to side.
2. When you have found the central place let your body settle in as you briefly hold your breath.
3. Exhale and feel that connection to Earth. Let your breath anchor your body.
4. Do the same as you rock your body from front to back and for all the parts of your body that you center.
5. When you are done and are sitting silently for the collection, feel your breath move slowly and evenly through your whole body.

Part Three – Connecting and Disconnecting

In the process of connecting, you make a connection with your surroundings and with Earth. You will need to visualize for this exercise. The idea is to see yourself connecting your energies to the space around you. I like to use the image of a tree. To begin this exercise, get into your sitting position.

Exercise 2.8 – The Tree

The image of a tree works very well for centering and connecting. Trees are tall and strong but can still move and be flexible when needed. This is the same way you will need to sit for meditation. Trees are very solid but they are not perfectly stiff. They can bend and rock slightly in the wind. See yourself the same way. You sit very still and solid but you are not completely frozen or stiff. You can move gently when it is needed but can remain still for a long time.

Chapter Two

Exercise no.	13 (2.8)
Goal	Connecting through the image of a tree
Minimum length of time	15 seconds
Location	anywhere
Needs	none
Steps	

1. Close your eyes in your sitting position. See your self as the trunk of a young tree.
2. Still seeing yourself as a tree, feel yourself growing roots below you. Let those roots extend deep into Earth and feel yourself connecting to the ground or surface below you. Feel yourself gaining strength and sustenance from the ground below you. If you are not directly connected to the ground let your roots grow until they do reach the ground and let them continue to sink in.
3. See yourself growing branches that reach high into the sky. Feel yourself spreading out against the sky touching the wind and growing leaves that drink in the sunshine or the moonlight. If it is raining or snowing you can still drink in the remaining light while you experience the touch of the precipitation falling around you.
4. When you have extended your reach above and below you, allow yourself to sit there and enjoy the experience for a few moments.
5. When you have finished, start to bring in your leaves and branches while keeping a feeling of flexible strength throughout your body. Then withdraw your roots until you feel that you will once again be ready to move about.

Exercise 2.9 – The Translucent Ball

Another image you can use for feeling connected is that of a clear or translucent ball of light or glow. This translucent ball is not just a boundary, it is living energy that connects with whatever it comes in contact.

Just Being

Exercise no.	14 (2.9)
Goal	To connect through the image of a ball of energy
Minimum length of time	15 seconds
Location	anywhere
Needs	none
Steps	

1. Begin by visualizing a translucent ball of energy in the center of your body.
2. As you breathe, let that ball of energy begin to slowly grow and expand until it fills your whole body. Let your breath be the engine for its growth.
3. Continue to breathe and allow the ball of energy become a sphere that surrounds you.
4. Continue to grow that sphere as it very gradually reaches down below you and up above. As your sphere grows, feel a connection between it and the Earth below as it descends and with the sky above as it ascends. Also feel a connection to the things around you in all directions.
5. Allow your breath to slowly begin the process of withdrawing the sphere until you bring it back to where you began.

Part Four – Entering In and Exiting

With this exercise you will create a space in your mind where you can go when you want to meditate. For some, it helps to create an inner temple or sanctuary that is completely their own and that can be visited when needed to find complete peace. Begin by sitting comfortably, relaxing completely, and closing your eyes.

Exercise 2.10 – The Inner Temple

In this exercise you will create and use a sacred space within your mind. I call that space the Inner Temple. It can be a place of refuge for you to go when you need it. You will begin from where you are and then transport yourself to a new place all your own. You may decide to ride a horse or a train or you might want to imagine something like a mysterious mist that magically transports you away.

Chapter Two

You might see a bridge or a rainbow or you might want to enter a dark cave. You could fly on the back of a magical creature or develop your own wings. You might ride a boat across a crystal clear mountain lake. As you move from here to there take time to enjoy the journey. You may see your house or local surroundings from above as you fly by or you may enter an entirely different tunnel of light and sounds. You choose for yourself what would be the most enjoyable way to travel. After a few moments, see yourself arriving at a magical place. Imagine what would be the most beautiful and most serene place for you. Take a few moments to clearly take in the surroundings of your new place. Look at all the details of the place. Observe the sky and the clouds. Take a good look at the plants, flowers, animals, and natural formations. Is there water in this place? Are there beautiful views and sights? What do you smell? What do you hear? What is the weather like?

When you have finished looking around, find an open space to build your temple or special place. Choose materials for your building or structure. Decide on a shape and build the structure with your mind. Carefully observe where you place the rooms, the doors, the windows, and other parts of the building. Make the place all your own – make it special. When it is done being built, enter inside and fill it with meaningful symbols and tools. Find a place to build an altar or a meditation space. Sit in that meditation space and enjoy the peace and tranquility of your new sacred inner temple. Enjoy your space for a time and, when you are ready, head back outside. Look again at the structure and at the surroundings of your special place. You will want to remember these things for the next time that you come to visit. Of course, you can change any details you like at any time but it helps to return to the place as you last remembered it. When you have finished taking a good look, start your journey back returning the same way in which you first came to this place. When you are ready open your eyes but keep a memory of your special place in your mind.

Just Being

Exercise no.	15 (2.10)
Goal	To create an inner safe and sacred space
Minimum length of time	1 minute
Location	anywhere
Needs	none
Steps	

1. See yourself in the space you are in.
2. Come up with a means of transportation and take it to your new location.
3. Arrive at your magickal place.
4. Create your inner temple.
5. Fill the interior of your temple with meaningful objects and symbols.
6. Sit and enjoy your space.
7. Exit your temple and return to the outside.
8. Return back using the same mode of transportation as before.

Part Five – Invocation and Release

The point of this exercise is to call upon the deities or powers you wish to bring to your meditation (if any). It is important to decide beforehand what entity or deity you wish to call upon. This decision should not be done during the meditation because you need a clear understanding of what you seek when you call to another power. Some Pagans choose to work with specific deities while others do not. Those who are the latter may wish to call upon specific energies or may wish to call upon Spirit, the higher self, or any positive energy.

A note about possibly negative experiences: it is possible to mistakenly call upon negative entities or energies. If at any time during this process you feel uncomfortable by the presence of something unknown, remember that you have the power to dismiss that entity from your space. That is why it is a good idea to create a virtual circle of protection around you either in this step or in any of the stretching routines that involve creating a magickal sphere. Allow only the energy that feels right to you to enter into that circle and know that you have the power to dismiss any unwanted energy at any time.

Exercise 2.11 – Invocation and Release

Start this meditation by seeing yourself in front of an actual or virtual altar. Create around you a magickal circle of protection in any manner that feels right to you. (Traditionally, the circle is cast in a clockwise direction and opened in a counter-clockwise direction.) Call upon your deity or entity to come protect and guide you as you enter into your meditation. You may choose to call upon a higher self or the power of love – whatever relates to your own spiritual practice. What you call upon is up to you and how you see your connection to the universe. Have a clear image in your mind of your deity or of a symbol that represents the entity or energy you seek. Feel the presence of this deity or energy around you. You might also offer a prayer or blessing at this time as a way of welcoming and honoring the deity invoked. Allow yourself a few moments to be in the presence of your entity and allow it to teach you or guide you as you feel comfortable. When you have finished, thank the entity and then ask it to leave. When the space around you is cleared, open and release your magickal circle and end your meditation.

Sample Invocation for Meditation

Spirit of the universe,
From both within and beyond,
I call upon you.
Help me seek to know and experience
Your wisdom and beauty through
This act of worship and prayer I call meditation.
Help me to see beyond the dark veil of separateness
Into the light of unity.
Show me that which I need to understand
In order to grow and help others.
Help me to be filled with your wisdom, love, and compassion.
Blessed Be.

Illustration 16: Meditation Invocation

Just Being

Exercise no.	16 (2.11)
Goal	Invoking a higher power
Minimum length of time	1 minute
Location	anywhere
Needs	none
Steps	

1. Get into your meditation position.
2. Create a magickal circle around you.
3. Call upon a higher power or concept.
4. Offer a prayer or blessing if you feel comfortable doing so.
5. Allow time to learn from the power.
6. Dismiss and thank the power.
7. End your meditation.

Part Six – Intent and Acknowledgment

The point of this exercise is to clearly state your intent before you begin your actual meditation practice. What happens before you do this exercise is probably more important than the exercise itself because you must first determine what the specific goal and focus of your meditation will be (even if that goal is to have an unfocused meditation). Before you begin any meditation, determine what exactly you hope to do and how you will work toward that goal. Think how you can clearly and distinctly state that goal to yourself. Only after you have done these things should you do this exercise.

Exercise 2.12 – Intent and Acknowledgment

After you have sat down, state clearly in your mind your intention for your meditation practice. For the purposes of this exercise, use something like the following statement: "I have come here to sit quietly and enjoy being completely relaxed for at least 10 minutes" (or whatever statement you prefer). This is my intent." You may say it aloud or say it silently to yourself but say it as if it were a royal proclamation being read to a crowd. Speak slowly and carefully. Feel the energy of the intent come from within you and fill your space. The intent should be made from your whole self. Experience it within your body, understand it with your mind, feel it in your heart, and allow it to be the connection between your soul and your deity or to Spirit.

When you have finished speaking, allow your body to relax completely. Breath with your whole body. Each time you breathe in, feel warmth and energy rise within you and each time you breathe out, allow that warmth and energy to fill your body and relax every muscle. Follow your breath as it moves through your body. If it helps you, think the words "breathe in joy" as you follow each breath entering your body and "breathe out tension" as you release each breath. Do this for what feels to be 10 minutes to you (regardless of whether or not 10 minutes really elapses). Then, offer a prayer or blessing of thanks for completing your meditation.

Acknowledge that you have made a connection to something beyond yourself. The energy you called upon to fill you is the energy of the universe – the breath of Spirit. By bringing it into yourself you recognize that you are part of a greater whole. Your breath (and water and food) comes from sources beyond yourself. You are part of a greater whole and your existence is dependent upon being part of that wholeness. Your life energy flows from the source of energy through you and through others as it returns to that source. Offering a prayer of thanks helps you to recognize that you are not a completely separate entity and that you are dependent on the love and help of others and of the universe.

Exercise no.	17 (2.12)
Goal	To clearly state your intent or meditation goal.
Minimum length of time	10 minutes
Location	anywhere
Needs	none
Steps	

1. Get into your meditation position.
2. Clearly state your intention for your practice.
3. Breathe in joy.
4. Breathe out tension.
5. Offer a blessing of thanks.
6. End your meditation.

Part Seven – Putting It All Together

In this exercise, you will put what you have learned in the previous exercises together into one exercise. As always, change whatever you need to make the exercise most effective for you. This exercise assumes that you have made all your preparations and have practiced all the previous exercises until you feel comfortable with each step. When you have finally put together a routine that feels best for you then be sure to practice it several times as a meditation practice until you feel comfortable and certain that you can do it with ease.

Exercise 2.13 – The Outer Meditation Procedure

Begin by doing the stretching routine you have chosen or developed. Then, sit down and come into your chosen meditation posture. Center your body and begin full body breathing. Connect yourself with the earth and sky using the image you have chosen. See in your mind your method of travel to your Inner Temple. Go to that place and enter into it. Create a sacred and safe circle around yourself in your mind. Call upon your deities or sources of inspiration or power and offer a prayer or blessing to do good work and to learn. Feel a connection to the universe. State clearly to yourself and the world your intention for your meditation work. Your intention for this exercise is simply to establish a regular meditation routine. Sit quietly for a moment and allow yourself to relax completely. Consider the procedure you just took and think about what did and did not feel right for you. Decide what you would like to change for the next time.

When you have finished, thank your deities or powers for assisting you and acknowledge your place in the universe. Ask your deities, energies, or powers to return. (Return may not be the best word since many Pagans believe that the sacred is within as well as beyond but the concept of engaging with the sacred may relate to the term as well.) Open your sacred circle and begin your return trip back from your Inner Temple. When you have returned, allow yourself to disengage from the earth and sky so that you will, once again, be free to move. You will still be connected on a psychic level but not a physical level. Take a moment to collect your thoughts about your experience and to enjoy this feeling of relaxation. When you are ready, open your eyes and stretch a bit. You have completed your outer meditation procedure.

I call this the Outer Procedure for there is yet another more subtle procedure to consider. This outer work prepares you to enter into a deep state of meditation. Though it can be done as one meditation itself, it is meant to lead to the inner working of a meditation practice. I urge you to practice this outer working as a meditation several times until it becomes an easy flowing process for you. Each time you practice it you should reduce it and refine it until it becomes a simple and quick procedure that will require little exertion. One way to help you do this is to come up with a procedure that works for you and then assign each part of that procedure a number going backwards to 1. For example, the steps you already learned in this chapter might look like the following:

6. Stretch
5. Center
4. Connect
3. Enter In
2. Invocation
1. Intention

Memorize the steps with the numbers and then use the numbers as a reminder for each step as you slowly work into your meditation. Count backwards as you begin and let each number remind you of the step to take. When you get to zero you will be ready to begin the inner work. When your meditation is ended use the same numbers in the opposite order to return.

1. Acknowledgment
2. Release
3. Exit
4. Disconnect
5. Collect
6. Stretch

Chapter Two

Exercise no.	18 (2.13)
Goal	To create a single outer meditation procedure.
Minimum length of time	5 minutes
Location	anywhere
Needs	none
Steps	

1. Count backwards from 6 assigning a past exercise with each number.
2. Do the exercise when you reach the number.
    1. Stretch (6)
    2. Center (5)
    3. Connect (4)
    4. Enter In (3)
    5. Invocation (2)
    6. Intention (1)
3. Sit for a few moments then begin the opposite process.
    1. Acknowledgment
    2. Release
    3. Exit
    4. Disconnect
    5. Collect
    6. Stretch
4. End your meditation

Just Being

Chapter Three
The Four Stages of Meditation
(The Inner Procedure)

Introduction

In this chapter I will explain what I call the four stages of meditation. These are stages that proceed from a light meditation to deeper levels of meditation by engaging all the parts of the self in the meditation practice. By progressing through these stages you can reach a deep level of meditation through what I call the Inner Procedure. As with the last chapter, each stage will be discussed separately at first and exercises will be provided for development. After each stage is developed you can then begin to create an Inner Procedure that helps you enter into each stage quickly. Take time to develop the skills and gain insight from working through each stage before trying to put them all together. The four stages of meditation are: Relaxation, Concentration, Acceptance, and Absorption and relate to engaging meditation through the body, mind, heart, and soul. In the first stage, the meditator completely relaxes the body. After finishing the relaxation phase, the meditator begins to focus on some object or concept to the exclusion of all other thoughts. The meditator next engages the heart by accepting him or herself and all other beings so that negative feelings will not interfere with the practice. I am not suggesting that there should be no feelings involved with meditation. Sometimes it is necessary to not ignore feelings and, instead, explore them as a process of growth but I am speaking of emotions that may interrupt or even disrupt your practice. In the final stage, the meditator continues to concentrate and block out other thoughts and feelings to such a high degree that he or she actually experiences a sense of union with the object of focus or with all of creation. This stage is called absorption and is the most exhilarating yet most challenging level of meditation.

The goal of this chapter is take an in-depth look at each of these stages and learn to develop the skills involved with each stage as separate practices. Once each has been practiced and developed, you will be asked to assign a mantra and a mudra for it. A *mantra* is a word or phrase that is used in many meditative practices as a focus for meditation. It is often repeated many times. A *mudra* is a specific hand position also used in many practices to induce a meditative frame of mind. With each completed stage we will assign both a mantra and a mudra to the experience so that you can quickly recall what you have learned and felt. When all four stages have been examined and practiced you will then be asked to put together a procedure that unites all the practices into one Inner Procedure.

Relaxation

Relaxation is the first level of meditation and it involves engaging the body. To begin any meditation practice, the entire body must be as relaxed as it can be while still allowing for awareness and focus. If your body is not to used to being relaxed on a regular basis then learning the skill may take some time and practice. You might also encounter some difficulties as you learn to relax. Letting go of tensions can cause you to come face to face with the cause of those tensions. Energy that is released in muscles can cause muscle tics and unusual sensations. Some people become warm when they relax while others feel cool. Relaxation may bring on feelings of exhaustion and a desire for sleep because the body may need more sleep after releasing long held tensions. Most of these problems are temporary and not difficult to overcome but it is important to be aware that they are possible.

There are many techniques for learning how to relax and you should, of course, find the one that works the best for you. I suggest that you first learn to relax lying down and then bring that feeling of relaxation into a sitting position. At all times it is important to remember how your body feels when it is in a state of relaxation so that you know what your goal is when you begin to relax again. Also, remembering the sensation of complete relaxation will act as a trigger to help you reach that state much faster each time you set out to relax.

One common relaxation method is called Progressive Relaxation in which each muscle of the body is consciously flexed and then released so that tension is released throughout the body. Usually the process is started at one end of the body and the person then progressively relaxes the other muscles in the body from that point. Using visualization is another good method for learning to relax the muscles. A comforting place can be used as a mental setting for encouraging relaxation. The Inner Temple is a good place to encourage a relaxed state of mind and body. Other useful techniques include: imagining your body as a pool of water or other natural images, following and observing the breath, or remembering a peaceful and comforting place such as the beach or a favorite camping spot. Our breathing naturally changes according to the state of relaxation in our bodies. In a state of relaxation, breathing is usually full and slow while in a state of panic breathing is usually erratic and shallow. You can encourage relaxation by simply slowing down the rate of your breathing. Concentrate on breathing with full slow breaths and stay with the breath as you feel your body relax.

Of course, just because you become relaxed does not necessarily mean that you will stay relaxed. It is easy to become distracted or agitated and allow tension to touch the body again. That is where the technique of the body scan becomes useful. A body scan is a quick mental scan of the body. You can constantly check the status of your relaxation by checking in with how each part of your body feels. If one part of your body still feels relaxed then move on to the next part and check how it feels. In this way, you can isolate each part of your body and be sure that every part is still relaxed.

Concentration

Concentration is the second stage of the Inner Procedure and involves the mind. Through concentration, an object of focus is chosen and then all thoughts are centered upon that object. The object of focus can be any number of things but the important idea is to keep the mind upon that object. The Buddhists call it "one-pointed mind."

All thoughts are centered upon one and only one thing during the meditation. The idea is to focus your mind in order to get past the mind. Most of us live in our heads; our Western culture focuses on thinking. We have developed great analytical and critical skills that do us very well in most instances but the spiritual involves all parts of the self. In order to connect with the spiritual we must be willing to embrace the mystery in all its facets. This requires us to go beyond the mind and into the great mystery. Since our mind is often the most active part of us we have to give it something to do while we go exploring beyond it. By constantly focusing on something your mind gets caught up in a focus loop.

Imagine that you are on one of those tour buses with a particularly chatty tour guide. Everywhere you go, this tour guide has to talk your ear off about whatever comes to her mind about whatever is just outside the bus window. Her voice constantly blares out over the bus P.A. System. You decide that you have had enough and come up with a plan to escape the endless commentary. At the next tour break, you ask the talkative tour guide to lead the bus in a rousing rendition of "99 Bottles of Beer." This is the song that starts singing about 99 bottles of beer on the wall and each time it is sung the number of bottles of beer is reduced by 1 until there are none left. Your trick is to have someone on the bus call out "99" every time the tour guide ends the first verse. In this way the same verse is sung over and over again. As the singing continues you manage to sneak away unnoticed by the distracted singing tour guide and go exploring on your own. This is similar to what you do as you concentrate on an object of focus. You are occupying your thinking mind while the rest of you explores the mystery beyond thought.

In order to begin the practice of concentration, it helps to first notice how busy your mind actually is. This can be done by observing the mind and using visualizations to get the mind to calm down a bit so that it can be set to work on concentrating. Next, an object of focus must be chosen. This object can be visual like a sacred object, a piece of art, a candle, sacred symbols, or even just a blank wall. Any single object can be used but it helps for that object to have some significance to your practice. This is why sacred symbols and objects work well. Some people use an altar when they meditate to place sacred objects and symbols upon it. Pagans have a variety of ways of constructing altars and any way that is significant to you is best. Some religions use a special work of art called a mandala which is designed specifically for meditation. The mandala is meant to draw you into the center of the piece through symbolism so that you can concentrate on that place in space. Some people use the imagery of the Tarot cards or symbols like the rune stones as a focus for concentration.

Once you have chosen your object of focus then you work to set your mind on only that object. All thoughts and attention must go onto that object to the exclusion of all else. This can be a very challenging practice if you are not used to doing it. As with many things, getting better requires practice and patience. It is important to be firm but forgiving in this work. If you find your mind drifting off to other subjects then gently guide it back to the focus. It is easy to become frustrated and angry towards yourself when this happens but anger only becomes yet another distraction. Imagine you are teaching a small child to ride a bicycle. You run along side her as she pedals to make sure she keeps moving forward. You know that if she drifts off the road she is likely to fall and hurt herself. As she starts to veer off, you gently take hold of the steering until she is again moving safely forward. As you help her you offer words of encouragement and hope. You know that if you started yelling at her or calling her names like "fool" or "stupid" she would only become angry and frustrated and might even crash and hurt herself. She might grip the handle bars more tightly and become even more erratic and frantic. Though many know that it would be harmful to yell at a child they are perfectly willing to yell at themselves. If you have trouble staying focused during your meditation, have patience and confidence in yourself. Instead of calling yourself names in frustration gently guide your mind back to its focus until it eventually learns to keep moving forward on its own. Keep your balance and keep pedaling.

Acceptance

Acceptance is the third stage of the Inner Procedure and involves the heart and emotions. Most meditation books talk about working with the body and the mind but stop there which, to me, leaves out the whole person. Acceptance is the ability to be comfortable with yourself and all else. There are three levels of

Just Being

acceptance: the self, all others, and the world. When meditating, it is important that you are comfortable being with the person who is doing the sitting. In other words, you need to be able to accept yourself for who you are. Imagine having to take a long airplane ride sitting next to someone who makes you feel nervous or uncomfortable. You could be in for a long and difficult trip; you might find it hard to relax or sleep. Something about this person just bothers you and you cannot ignore it. You toss and turn and wish that you were somewhere – anywhere - else. Some people are just as uncomfortable sitting with themselves as they are sitting next to a disturbing passenger. They simply cannot relax while being alone or they have a very low image of themselves which makes them hyper-critical of their own actions. Every moment alone is spent listening to a belligerent inner voice.

We are part of the cycles of life and our striving to be who we are assures that we are part of these cycles.

At some point in every life, a person has to come to accept the fact that we are all fallible. We are human and we are not meant to be perfect. If we were, we would all be the same. Imagine a world with a bunch of purely perfect people walking about. How boring and dull! We are meant to struggle and be different. We are part of the cycles of life and our striving to be who we are assures that we are part of these cycles. Spirit lives through us in these constant struggles and spirals of renewal. Accept that at this moment in time you may be exactly who you should be. Of course there are always things that can be done better but you have to start somewhere and that somewhere is here and now. Become who you will be by starting with who you are now. If you can do this then you can be comfortable with that passenger sitting beside you on the flight because that person may be yourself.

Accepting yourself is only the first level of acceptance, however. In reality we are all on the same flight and every day we come face to face with different passengers. There will always be those out there who want to do you harm just as there will always be those out there who wish you no harm at all. The second level of acceptance is learning to accept others for who they are. I am not saying that you should love everyone – that may be asking too much. Accepting someone does not require that you like that person. It only requires that you respect others and have no desire to try and change them into something else. Spending time wishing that others thought, acted, or looked like you is a waste of energy and time. You are who you are and they are who they are – it is as simple as that. You may be able to sit in meditation much easier when you can stop worrying about why people do not like you or why is it that everyone else is so crazy.

The third level of acceptance is to learn to accept your place in the universe. Just as other people are not going to always conform to your wishes, neither is the universe. The weather may be disagreeable, you may be getting older, there may be wars around the world, but there is very little that you can do about any of these things. You will find peace of mind when you can learn to accept the things that you cannot change and that peace of mind is necessary if you hope to find an inner peace during meditation. This does not mean that you should never do anything to try and make yourself and the world better. On the contrary, if you discover something that you can do to make a positive change for the world, then you should do it. Wisdom comes from recognizing what it is you have the power to change and what it is that you cannot change and then learning to accept both.

Absorption

Absorption is the fourth and most difficult stage of meditation since it relates to the soul and to our connection with Spirit. Absorption takes place when we become so in tune with the object of concentration that we actually become at one with it. This is sometimes called *flow*. In the midst of absorption, you and the object of concentration merge until all sense of separation is gone. You literally lose yourself. Some people experience a sense of rapture in flow while others are not able to take note of their feelings until much later. There is a sense that all time stops and that there is nothing but the present – the eternal now. The idea of finding yourself within a certain space becomes meaningless. There is only the here and the now and nothing else.

There are really two kinds of absorption although they both

achieve the same goal. In the digital world we can understand these two states as 1 or 0. Oneness is the experience of expansion while zero-ness is the experience of dissolution. In the first type of absorption, everything merges into one thing (the one). All things become a unified whole in an ever-present now. In the second state, all things disappear until there is nothing (the 0 or void). In this state, all things cease to be active and you become part of the nothingness that fills all things. The Tao Te Ching explains this emptiness as the space that fills the cup or the emptiness that makes a room possible. At first, these concepts seem ridiculous. How can one experience totality or pure emptiness? I can only say that it is possible. It is very difficult to aptly describe these states since they go beyond what words can depict. They must be experienced directly by the meditator in order to be truly understood. Ultimately, the two states are really two experiences of the same thing. All things are nothing and nothing is in all things. This seems like a paradox but learning to understand this truth can help you begin to understand the mysteries of the universe.

In order to experience absorption you must first have been successful at the previous three stages of meditation. Your body must be completely relaxed, your mind must be empty and free of distracting thoughts, and your heart must be open and free of anger and hatred. In other words, there must be nothing that will distract your body, mind, and heart, but your soul also must be free of distractions as well. That is done by freeing any obstacles which would allow you to connect to whatever is your sense of the Ultimate Reality. If you are unsure what that is to you then you will not be able to make a connection. It is like picking up the phone and not knowing who to call. Through your Pagan practice you will need to define your understanding of Spirit by whatever name or method you choose to use. Once you know with whom or what you are connecting on the other side of the phone line you then need to consider the quality of the connection. If you decided to call your best friend but did so on a poor quality phone or one with a bad connection you might not be able to have a worthwhile conversation regardless of how well you knew your friend. The quality of your connection to the universe depends on how you view that connection. If you think you are not worthy of relating to the divine then your connection will be weak. Remember that all beings are equal in Spirit. There is no one person or being less

Chapter Three

than another. Period. All are part of and are the manifestation of Spirit. You have the same worth and value as any other person. Spirit is that true inner essence of yourself. If you can connect to the inner self then you can connect to Spirit.

Conversely, there are some who believe that they do not need any connection to something beyond the everyday self. Such people will have difficulty with this stage of meditation because they will only be able to be absorbed by their own selves. Absorption requires that you connect with something else. In the dissolution process, the meditator completely forgets herself. Like many children, I had a favorite blanket growing up and it was difficult to let that blanket go when the time came but I knew I had to do it in order to grow up. That blanket and I had seen a lot of times together and it was always there when I needed it. But, at some point I knew I had to let it go. The same is true of the concept of the self. We cling on to our image of ourselves like a comforting blanket but, at times, we need to be able to let it go so that we can grow. There is something more powerful and strong at the core of your being but you have to be willing to let go of the outer layers to see it. You can compare it to a sunflower with many petals that is waiting for the sun to rise so that it can open up to the warmth and light. Only with patience and calmness will that flower eventually open. In the process of expansion you can focus on yourself but in a way that allows the image of yourself to envelop all things. This process requires that you change your identity from a single being to a being that includes all others. Like the alien creature in the movie *The Blob*, you need to allow the concept of yourself to grow and embrace everything around you until there is no difference between you and everything else. Unlike the blob, however, there will be no dividing line between you and all else (and, presumably, you are not an evil alien creature).

Even though absorption may be a difficult stage to reach in your meditative practice, I believe it is very important. One of the disadvantages of meditation is that it can make one become too self-focused. A meditator may have all kinds of wonderful experiences and insights, reach new levels of relaxation, mental concentration, and emotional awareness but have absolutely no sense that there is anything beyond the self. For me, the definition of spirituality is that which connects you to something beyond yourself - even if that thing beyond you is also within you. As a Pagan, that thing for me is Spirit and is the energy that is the source and essence of all creatures and all things. For me, Spirit is both within and beyond us. It is the energy that is the essence of all things as discovered by Albert Einstein ($E=MC^2$). More than just a stream of electrons waiting to be used to fire up your toaster, this energy is a form of consciousness – not a human consciousness - but an all encompassing awareness of the ever present here and now. Connecting to Spirit helps me feel a sense of connection to all people, all creatures, all living things, and all inanimate objects and allows me to experience the here and now. It is a humbling feeling, to say the least. Absorption is the stage of meditative practice that brings you out of yourself so that you not only understand your connection with all things, you actually experience that unity.

Combining the Stages

As in the Outer Procedure discussed in the previous chapter, the Inner Procedure will combine all the things you have learned in this chapter. The separate practices will all be combined to make a single procedure. The key to doing this will be to carefully monitor and remember the experiences developed from the practice of each of the four stages. Then, each will be assigned a one word mantra that will be used to associate the feeling with that word. When you repeat that word in your mind it should call back those feelings and help you remember what the successful completion of each stage felt like. In this way, you can quickly recall the work you did. I encourage you to choose whatever words best suit you and your practice but I will use four specific words in this text. Each stage will also be given a mudra or hand position that will also serve as a reminder to your body of your experiences with each stage. With the four mantras you can then create a single set of hand motions that bring you quickly through the four stages and prepare you for your meditative work.

Summary

The second procedure to be learned for meditation is what I call the Inner Procedure and helps you focus on developing the four

Chapter Three

levels of meditation each of which are associated with a part of the self. Relaxation is the first stage and deals with the body. Concentration is the second stage and concerns using the mind to center all thought on an object of focus. The third level is called Acceptance because it deals with learning to accept yourself and all other beings through the heart while the fourth stage, Connection deals with the soul and its connection to that which is beyond and within the self. Each stage should be approached and practiced separately until some mastery is gained into reaching that stage easily and quickly. To help do that, a mantra and a mudra is chosen to remind yourself quickly how each stage felt. When all four levels have been mastered they are then put together into one procedure.

Exercises

This section contains several exercises for you to try. Each will be focused on developing the four stages individually and then, as we did with the Outer Procedure, the four stages will be combined into one procedure. The first exercises will begin by having you lie down but all subsequent exercises should be done in your sitting position and should be preceded by your Outer Procedure. Some people prefer to meditate with music. If this is the case, be sure to choose music that will not distract you and have it set up so you will not have to interrupt your practice in order to fiddle with the music player. Also, it would be better to find a longer piece of music to enjoy rather than several short selections that might disturb your meditative experience.

Part One – Relaxation

The first exercises will focus on progressive relaxation which encourage you to think of each part of your body separately as you relax. Starting from your feet, you slowly progress the relaxation up and through your body. Allowing your mind to visualize images of relaxation or to think about parts of your body will help you learn to more fully relax. As you learn the steps to relaxation, you will then connect the breath to the process so that the inhalation brings in relaxation deep into the body and the exhalation releases tension. You will also learn how to do a body scan which is a quick mental scan you do to search the body for unnecessary tension. Finally, you will learn to do a deep relaxation through a visualization that will release all tension throughout the body after which you will seek out a mantra to use to remind your body of these exercises.

Exercise 3.1 – Tensing Muscles

Begin by lying down in a comfortable position. I recommend you lie on the floor if it is comfortable rather than your bed or couch simply because your body may be used to sleeping in the bed or couch. Make the place you are using as comfortable as possible. You will do this exercise by flexing and squeezing and then quickly releasing the muscles of each part of your body beginning from your feet. It is important that you squeeze the muscles as hard as you can and hold that flexed muscle for several seconds (before it becomes painful) and then suddenly release that muscle as quick as possible.

Exercise no.	19 (3.1)
Goal	Relaxing muscles through tensing and releasing them.
Minimum length of time	10 minutes
Location	anywhere
Needs	none
Steps	

1. Begin your meditation with your outer procedure steps 1-6. (Chapter Two)
2. Lie down in a comfortable place
3. Flex each muscle in the order listed below.
4. Release that same muscle quickly and feel the relaxed sensation.
5. Continue the process upwards through your body.
6. After you have finished, lie quietly and enjoy the relaxation.
7. End your meditation with the outer procedure steps 8-13.

Chapter Three

> **Parts of the Body**
>
> 1. feet
> 2. legs
> 3. stomach and hips
> 4. upper chest and shoulders
> 5. hands and arms
> 6. face and neck
> 7. whole body

Illustration 17: Parts of the Body

Exercise 3.2 – Visualization

In this exercise, you will lie down and concentrate on each part of your body. In the same order as above, imagine that each part of your body becomes slowly warm and heavy as if you were filling it with a warm liquid like wax or warm water. Use whatever image best works for you. Begin with your feet. Imagine that your feet become filled with a warm liquid or maybe a golden light that reminds you of the warmth of the sun. Let this feeling of warmth fill your feet. As it does, allow your feet to also feel very heavy – as if they were weighed down to the ground and would be very difficult for you to lift. Allow this liquid or light to move very slowly through your body in the order listed above. Slowly, your entire body should become very warm and heavy until you feel as if you could not move or lift anything. You should feel completely connected to the floor. Feel the sensation of complete relaxation. Remember what it feels like so you can recall it again later. When you are ready to end the exercise, allow the liquid or light to drain away from your body so that it may become light again. Though the heaviness is drained away, the sense of relaxed comfort may remain. When the liquid or light has been drained off, you should be ready to slowly sit up and end this exercise.

Exercise no.	20 (3.2)
Goal	To relax the body progressively through visualization.
Minimum length of time	10 minutes
Location	anywhere
Needs	none
Steps	

1. Begin your meditation with your outer procedure steps 1-6.
2. Lie down comfortably
3. Fill each part of your body with an imaginary warm liquid.
4. Continue until your whole body feels warm and relaxed.
5. Let the liquid drain until you feel light and relaxed.
6. End your meditation with the outer procedure steps 8-13.

Exercise 3.3 – Progressive Relaxation I: Sitting

In this and all exercises from this point you should begin by getting into your sitting posture. This exercise combines the previous two but is done in the sitting position so that you will be ready to meditate. From your sitting position, concentrate on each part of your body in the order listed above. Tense each part tightly and then release it. As you release the muscle allow the warm liquid or light to enter it and fill it so that it becomes heavy and warm. Do this up through your body to each area. You may need to tense the muscles differently sitting up but the exercise will still be effective. When you have finished doing each area, sit quietly and enjoy the relaxed sensation until you are ready to drain the liquid or light and complete the exercise.

Chapter Three

Exercise no.	21 (3.3)
Goal	To apply the relaxation technique to a sitting position.
Minimum length of time	10 minutes
Location	anywhere
Needs	none
Steps	

1. Do your outer meditation procedure steps 1-6.
2. Get into your sitting position.
3. Tense and release each part of your body.
4. As you do so, visualize a warm liquid or gentle light entering your body.
5. Enjoy the relaxed feeling.
6. End your meditation with the outer procedure steps 8-13.

Exercise 3.4 – Progressive Relaxation II: Breathing

Do the above exercise (1C) once again but with the following change. As you concentrate on each part of the body, let your breathe direct the flow of the warm liquid or light. For example, as you focus on relaxing your feet also focus on your breathe. On the inhalation feel as if you were breathing all the way into your feet. Allow the inhalation to slowly pull the liquid or light into your feet a little bit at a time. With each exhalation, feel the tension in your feet being whisked away as a breeze might blow dirt off your porch. Each inhalation pulls in more liquid or light and each exhalation releases tension. Do this throughout your whole self until you feel as if you can breathe with your entire body.

Just Being

Exercise no.	22 (3.4)
Goal	To add breathing to the relaxation process.
Minimum length of time	10 minutes
Location	anywhere
Needs	none
Steps	

1. Begin your meditation with your outer procedure steps 1-6.
2. Get into your sitting position.
3. Begin breathing fully.
4. With each inhalation begin to fill your body with a warm liquid or light.
5. Continue until you fill your whole body.
6. Enjoy the relaxation.
7. Slowly drain or release the liquid or light until all is gone.
8. End your meditation with the outer procedure steps 8-13.

Exercise 3.5 – The Body Scan

The body scan is a quick way for you to check in with your body and make sure that it is completely relaxed. If you have ever gone shopping and seen one of those price scanners you may have noticed the thin red laser line that is used to read the bar code on your product. Imagine that you also can produce a thin laser line that is spread horizontally across your body. Allow that thin line to begin below your feet and slowly work its way up your body. As it moves, concentrate on that part of your body and check to see if it still feels as relaxed as it was when you did the relaxation exercises above. Use your memory of how that relaxation felt to return that feeling to each area. If there is tension then release it. Continue through the rest of your body and do the same process. Do this body scan periodically throughout your meditation.

Chapter Three

Exercise no.	23 (3.5)
Goal	To check on the relaxation level of your body.
Minimum length of time	10 minutes
Location	anywhere
Needs	none
Steps	

1. Begin your meditation with your outer procedure steps 1-6.
2. Get into your sitting position.
3. Scan your body from feet to head.
4. Notice if any part is experiencing tension. If so, release that tension.
5. Continue the scan throughout your body.
6. End your meditation with the outer procedure steps 8-13.

Exercise 3.6 – Deep Relaxation

This exercise takes the progressive relaxation exercises one step further to encourage a very deep level of relaxation. The first time you do this exercise you may wish to lie down but try to do it sitting up several times after you have experienced it once. Begin by doing the progressive relaxation above. Tense and relax each part of the body. Then, use your visualization powers and slowly fill each part of your body with the warm liquid or light. Connect the visualization with your breath. Your body should be very relaxed. Now, release the breath. Allow the breath to continue on its own just as the wind blows on its own. You are breathing with your whole body so you do not need to take large amounts of air. Instead, your breathing should, by itself, become very slow and shallow like a gentle summer breeze. The next step will depend on which image you used for your visualization. If, for example, you are using the image of a warm liquid like wax then you should visualize that your body is now completely and comfortably filled with this warm liquid. It is a magickal liquid, of course, so you do not feel the least bit constricted. Vision yourself on the floor as this large clump of wax. Slowly allow the wax to melt completely until there is only a pool of melted liquid on the floor. If you use the light image, allow the light to slowly seep out the pores of your skin until you completely become pure light. Another image that can be used is the image of a lake. Imagine that as you begin this exercise you are like a lake or pond whose surface is choppy and moving. As you continue the exercise, slowly allow the surface of the water to become still until it becomes as clear and motionless as glass. Whichever image you use, be sure to allow yourself to enjoy this sense of deep relaxation and to remember how it feels so that you can easily recall it again.

Exercise no.	24 (3.6)
Goal	To take the relaxation procedure even further by encouraging a deeper state of relaxation.
Minimum length of time	10 minutes
Location	anywhere
Needs	none
Steps	

1. Begin your meditation with your outer procedure steps 1-6.
2. Get into your sitting position.
3. Fill each part of your body with a warm liquid or light.
4. Allow that liquid to completely melt or become pure light.
5. Enjoy the experience of being completely relaxed.
6. Return your body to its normal self.
7. End your meditation with the outer procedure steps 8-13.

Exercise 3.7 – The Relaxation Mantra

Choose a word that you would like to use as a trigger for your body to remember how it feels to be relaxed. I will use the word *relax* but you should choose whatever word is best for you. This word will be your mantra. To begin, repeat the above exercises and go into a deep relaxation. In that relaxed state begin to repeat in your mind your mantra. Try to do this for several minutes. If your mind begins to drift, simply begin the mantra again. Remember to be kind to yourself; it is all right if you have trouble doing this at first. Like any other skill, it must be practiced. Whenever you say that mantra to yourself it should immediately bring back the feelings of relaxation you experienced in your exercises.

Exercise no.	25 (3.7)
Goal	To attach a word trigger to the experience of relaxation.
Minimum length of time	10 minutes
Location	anywhere
Needs	mantra word
Steps	

1. Begin your meditation with your outer procedure steps 1-6.
2. Get into your sitting position.
3. Begin repeating your relaxation mantra.
4. Recall how it feels to be completely relaxed.
5. End your meditation with the outer procedure steps 8-13.

Exercise 3.8 – The Relaxation Mudra

Choose a position to help remind your body of its ability to relax completely. I suggest moving your hands out to your sides at about the distance of your shoulders. Turn your palms up and bring your index fingers to your thumbs until they touch and form a circle. Some people place the backs of their palms upon their knees. This is a popular mudra for Buddhists and is often used during their meditations. Once again, do the above exercises to relax fully. Form your mudra and begin repeating your mantra for several moments. Do this only for as long as you can remain relaxed and focused on your meditation.

Exercise no.	26 (3.8)
Goal	To attach a hand position to the relaxation experience.
Minimum length of time	10 minutes
Location	anywhere
Needs	hand position
Steps	

1. Begin your meditation with your outer procedure steps 1-6.
2. Get into your sitting position.
3. Bring your hands into your relaxation mudra.
4. Begin your relaxation mantra.
5. Experience the connection of complete relaxation to your mudra and mantra.
6. End your meditation with the outer procedure steps 8-13.

Part Two – Concentration

Through the following concentration exercises you will learn to more intently focus upon a particular goal. We will begin by simply learning to open and calm the mind. From that point, we will practice concentrating on many different subjects including visual, aural, mental, and physical means. For each of these exercises you should first become completely relaxed. Use your relaxation mantra and mudra to get you quickly to that state of complete relaxation.

Exercise 3.9 – Observing the Mind

In this exercise you will just sit and watch your mind. It will be like the loving parent in the yard watching the child play. You will simply watch your mind as it scatters about. The object here is to not just let the mind wander but to closely observe it as it wanders. You should ask yourself: what is my mind thinking about? Where does it wander? What does it fixate upon? Are my thoughts mostly positive or negative? Do I focus on daily life and stresses or do I mostly dream about other things? This exercise is sometimes called The Witness Meditation because you are separating yourself into two parts: one is the person you are during the day and the second is the silent watchful witness who observes and takes note of what the other part is doing. You can do this exercise throughout the day to begin to observe how you think and act around others and in your daily activities.

Exercise no.	27 (3.9)
Goal	To observe without judgment the workings of the mind.
Minimum length of time	10 minutes
Location	anywhere
Needs	none
Steps	

1. Begin your meditation with your outer procedure steps 1-6.
2. Get into your sitting position.
3. Relax your body.
4. Let your mind begin to wander.
5. As it does so, observe it and where it tends to go.
6. End your meditation using the outer procedure steps 8-13.

Exercise 3.10 – Clearing the Mind

With this exercise, you will practice emptying the mind through a visualization. Get into your sitting position and relax. Imagine that you are in a house. This is a special house because it is actually yourself that you will be entering. Work your way upstairs to the attic. This attic is your mind. In this attic there is a lot of clutter and dust. On both sides of the attic there is a small window to the outside. I want you to clear the dust by opening the small windows. This dust represents all your daily thoughts and worries that are not processed. Let the dust escape through the windows and feel yourself release these little scraps of worry. Remember that meditation time is *your* time so you do not need these little worries and fears right now. You can release them for as long as you meditate. Next, organize your attic so it is not so cluttered. These things are the bigger worries and fears of your life. You can not so easily discard these but you can pack them away in the far corner of your attic at least while you are meditating. Now, sit back between the windows. Imagine that any thought that enters into your mind is like a breeze that comes into one of the windows. Allow it to come in one window and then exit through the other. In this way, your thoughts may continue but you will not allow them to stop and be processed. Just let them come and go as a an occasional breeze might swirl in and out of the attic. If you stop to consider a thought that comes your way your windows will slam shut and it will become stuffy again. If that happens, just open the windows once more and let the attic clear out. With some practice, you will develop the discipline to not engage the thoughts that enter your mind but will be able to just observe them coming in and going away.

Exercise no.	28 (3.10)
Goal	To avoid attachment to the flow of incoming thoughts.
Minimum length of time	10 minutes
Location	anywhere
Needs	none
Steps	

1. Begin your meditation with your outer procedure steps 1-6.
2. Get into your sitting position.
3. Relax your body.
4. Visualize your mind as an attic in a house.
5. Open the side windows and allow the attic and your mind to clear.
6. Allow thoughts to just come and go through the windows.
7. End your meditation with the outer procedure steps 8-13.

Exercise 3.11 – Relaxing the Mind

Just as you did with your body, you can also learn to relax your mind. You can tense the mind by forcing yourself to think as many thoughts as you can as fast as you can and all at once. Try to think of as many things as possible that worry you or call for your attention throughout the day. Make a mental list of everything that you could possibly think about – especially those things which frustrate you and take up mental energy. Go through your list of worries, needs, and frustrations and burn through as many of them as you can and as fast as you can. Then, suddenly release those thoughts and completely clear your mind. Enjoy this peace of mind for as long as you can hold it. If thoughts begin to return then repeat the process.

Exercise no.	29 (3.11)
Goal	Applying the physical relaxation procedure to the mind.
Minimum length of time	10 minutes
Location	anywhere
Needs	none
Steps	

1. Begin your meditation with your outer procedure steps 1-6.
2. Get into your sitting position.
3. Relax your body.
4. Flex your mind by thinking as many random thoughts as possible.
5. Suddenly release those thoughts and empty your mind.
6. Try to maintain the empty mind for as long as possible.
7. If necessary, repeat steps 4 and 5 again.
8. End your meditation with the outer procedure steps 8-13.

Exercise 3.12 – Visual Concentration

This exercise is designed to get you to focus on a visual object. That object can be anything but the most powerful objects to focus upon are those that have special meaning to you. A religious symbol, an image or picture of a deity, a spiritual object, or a special candle are just a few of the things that can work well. Another useful object is a mandala which is an artistic work that is specifically designed to help with meditation. Mandalas often draw you into the center of their design in the same way that meditation draws you into your own center.

Just Being

Illustration 18: An Example of a Mandala

Begin by getting into your sitting position and fully relaxing. Set your complete attention upon your visual object of focus. As you continue to look at it allow your mind to open. Carefully look at every detail of the object. Notice how each separate thing is unique and beautiful. Notice how each part relates to all the others. Switch from seeing details to seeing the whole object. Follow every line and every curve. Seek to find hidden shapes or meanings. Look for symbolic associations throughout. Put yourself completely into the object. When you have finished, close your eyes for a while and allow them to rest.

Exercise no.	30 (3.12)
Goal	To use a mantra as a focus for concentration.
Minimum length of time	10 minutes
Location	anywhere
Needs	mandala
Steps	

1. Begin your meditation with your outer procedure steps 1-6.
2. Get into your sitting position.
3. Relax your body.
4. Allow your mind to focus on the mandala..
5. See both the details and the totality of the design.
6. Focus on the meanings of the design.
7. Allow yourself to enter into the center.
8. Later, withdraw from the center.
9. End your meditation using the outer procedure steps 8-13.

Exercise 3.13 – Aural Concentration: Music

Many people enjoy listening to music during their meditations but music can be more than pleasant background noise. It can also be the central focus of your meditation. It is important to find music that is soothing and meaningful to you. Many prefer compositions that are slow moving and calming rather than hard and fast for meditation. To use music as the focus of your concentration you will need to find something that really touches and is meaningful to you. Next, you will need a good quality stereo system with good speakers or a good pair of headphones. A poor reproduction of your music will be distracting and useless to you. You need to be able to hear every subtle detail of the music you have chosen. Just as you did with the visual exercise, allow yourself to become immersed in the music as you listen. Hear both the complexity and beauty of the work as a whole while also seeking to hear every small detail of the sounds. Listen for connections and meaning. Allow your emotions to be linked with the music and let them go where they may. Let go and become completely immersed in the experience of the melodies, harmonies, and rhythms. Hear how each instrument sounds by itself and with the other instruments. Notice how the music takes shape and form. Try not to analyze. There is nothing you need to think about or synthesize. Just be part of the journey.

Exercise no.	31 (3.13)
Goal	To use music as a focus for concentration.
Minimum length of time	10 minutes
Location	anywhere
Needs	music and a music player
Steps	

1. Begin your meditation with your outer procedure steps 1-6.
2. Get into your sitting position.
3. Relax your body.
4. Begin listening to a piece of music.
5. Let the music connect to you.
6. When the music ends, end your meditation using the outer procedure steps 8-13.

Exercise 3.14 – Aural Concentration: Chanting

Making your own music can also be a powerful method of meditation – especially if you use a chant. A chant is a short musical phrase that is repeated and usually has a sacred text. You can turn any meaningful phrase into a chant simply by repeatedly singing it. Melodies with small ranges and simple rhythms often work best. The Hindus have a long tradition of chanting on the word "om" (or "aum"). The word is used to focus thoughts and energies inward. Moving from an open "oh" sound to the closed "mm" sound draws you inward and the final sound causes a vibration in the body. This vibration is considered to be the same vibration that began and exists throughout the universe. Hindus believe that the world was created from sound and that we can attune to that same primordial sound through meditation.

In your relaxed sitting position, began to breathe fully and slowly. After taking several full breaths begin the exhalation by chanting an "oh" sound. The specific pitch you sing on does not matter and will probably change. Each time you do this exercise your body

Chapter Three

may find the pitch that is needed. Part of the point of this exercise is to let go and allow your body to do just that. Different vibrations will affect different parts of your body and your mind so allow yourself to change pitch according to what your body tells you. Some people start on a low pitch and then "scoop" upward until a comfortable pitch is reached. Do the "oh" sound several times. Make sure your body, especially the throat area, remains completely relaxed. Then, add the "mm" sound. As you bring your lips together allow the pitch to vibrate first in your neck and head and then throughout your whole body. Allow this vibration to gently massage and heal your body. Continue to chant with the motion of your breath. Breathe in slowly and then breathe out by chanting the "om" sound. If you begin to feel light headed, stop the chant for a few breaths until you feel better and then begin again. Let yourself enjoy some silence and the effects of the soothing vibration for a while after you finish this exercise.

Exercise no.	32 (3.14)
Goal	To use chanting as the focus for concentration.
Minimum length of time	10 minutes
Location	anywhere
Needs	none
Steps	

1. Begin your meditation with your outer procedure steps 1-6.
2. Get into your sitting position.
3. Relax your body.
4. Breathe in fully.
5. As you exhale, chant the "om" sound.
6. Let the vibrations connect to your body.
7. Continue for several minutes.
8. End your meditation with the outer procedure steps 8-13.

Exercise 3.15 – Aural Concentration: The Bell

Another method used by many traditions is to listen to the sound of a bell. Strike the bell once lightly to get it to begin to vibrate and then strike it again a little harder. Listen to the sound of the bell as it fades away. Try to maintain the sound of the bell in your mind so that it actually continues to ring within you. Continue for as long as you can hear the ring.

Exercise no.	33 (3.15)
Goal	To use the continuous ring of a bell as the focus for concentration.
Minimum length of time	10 minutes
Location	anywhere
Needs	a beautiful sounding bell
Steps	

1. Do your outer meditation procedure using steps 1-6.
2. Get into your sitting position.
3. Ring your bell once lightly to get it vibrating.
4. Ring it again more firmly.
5. Concentrate on the fading sound of the bell.
6. Let the sound continue within you.
7. When you can no longer hear the bell, either ring it again or end your meditation using the outer procedure steps 8-13.

Exercise 3.16 – Contemplation: Who Am I?

The next three exercises will focus on using the mind as a method for concentration. The idea is to set the mind on a single repetitive task until it breaks through its normal mode of thinking. In this first exercise you will be asked to think upon a single question that has a difficult answer. After getting into your relaxed sitting position you should begin asking yourself the question "Who am I?" At first you will answer the question with common labels like "I am a father" or "I am a computer programmer" or "I am a Pagan" but none of these really answers the question. You want to discover the real essence of who you are. It is fine to explore your roles in life such as the ones I just mentioned but the real answer to the question goes beyond these labels. Like an actor who wears many masks, we have many identities in our lives but the question "Who am I" asks us to go beyond those masks and identify the actor within. To find the answer you must find the you that speaks the words and thinks the thoughts. You must find the you that has no face and no body yet fills the body and the face. You must find the source of your loves and sorrows, fears and pains, joys and frustrations. The answer to the question "Who am I" will lead you to the inner core of the self. It will lead you to find the person you were before you were born and the person you will be after you die. Contemplate on this simple question and look beyond labels, expectations, and limitations.

Exercise no.	34 (3.16)
Goal	To use contemplation on the identification of the self as a focus for concentration.
Minimum length of time	10 minutes
Location	anywhere
Needs	none
Steps	

1. Begin your meditation with your outer procedure steps 1-6.
2. Get into your sitting position.
3. Relax your body.
4. Consider the question "Who am I?"
5. Continue asking the question until you get to the true essence of who you are.
6. Consider the implications of your answers to the question.
7. End your meditation with the outer procedure steps 8-13.

Exercise 3.17 – Contemplation: Sacred Reading

Another thought meditation method is to find a sacred text and contemplate upon passages within it. You can use most any work that is meaningful to you but sacred scriptures often work very well. Books like the Bible, the Koran, the Tao Te Ching, or the Dhammapada can provide plenty of unique viewpoints about living in the world. I like to use the Tao Te Ching because it has very short readings but its texts are often very challenging since they deal with seemingly contradictory ideas. For example, the first reading says that the Tao (the Taoist term for the ultimate reality) is that which cannot be named. How can you name something (the Tao) and then say it has no name? If you do not just ignore the question and say it is simply ridiculous and not worth your time, then you will miss the chance to find an answer that will lead you to insights about the mysteries of the world.

Find a sacred text that is meaningful to you and let yourself enter into a meditative state before you read it. Then, read it slowly until you find a passage that you can begin to contemplate upon. Let that contemplation be your meditation and allow yourself to freely explore all the insights and meanings that may come from exploring that passage.

Exercise no.	35 (3.17)
Goal	To use a sacred reading as a focus for concentration.
Minimum length of time	10 minutes
Location	anywhere
Needs	a sacred text
Steps	

1. Begin your meditation with your outer procedure steps 1-6.
2. Get into your sitting position.
3. Relax your body.
4. Begin reading a sacred or important text you have chosen.
5. Contemplate upon specific passages.
6. End your meditation using the outer procedure steps 8-13.

Exercise 3.18 – Contemplation: The Silent Om

This exercise is similar to the chanting exercise in 10B except that the "om" sound is done internally. Instead of actually chanting the sound vocally, internalize the sound in your mind. You can connect it with the breath or you can continue the humming part of the "om" chant (the "mm" sound) indefinitely. The difficulty of this exercise is that it takes even more concentration to maintain the inner sound but the advantage is that you do not have to interrupt the chant with the breath. Try to maintain a continuous humming sound for as long as you can. If you begin to drift off in your thoughts or concentration, take a deep breath and begin the "om" again. Imagine that your entire body vibrates with the hum and that the vibration in your body is the same as the underlying vibration of the universe.

Exercise no.	36 (3.18)
Goal	To use the sound of an inner "om" as a focus for concentration.
Minimum length of time	10 minutes
Location	anywhere
Needs	none
Steps	

1. Begin your meditation with your outer procedure steps 1-6.
2. Get into your sitting position.
3. Relax your body.
4. Begin a continuous "om" sound in your mind.
5. Concentrate fully on the sound.
6. Continue for several minutes.
7. End your meditation using the outer procedure steps 8-13.

Exercise 3.19 – Mindfulness

Mindfulness is an important meditation exercise in many Buddhist practices. It is a physical exercise in that you learn to meditate while engaging your body in an activity. Any activity will do but the more mundane it is, the better. Thich Nhat Hanh uses the example of washing the dishes. In his treatise, he explains how you can be totally in the present moment while doing the dishes by concentrating your thoughts entirely on the activity. When you wash the dishes, think about only what you are currently doing. Fill your mind with thoughts like "I am rinsing the dish," "I am washing the dish," or "I am drying the dish." Think about how your hands feel, how the dishes feel, how the soap smells and feels, the sound of the dishes clinking together, and so on. Focus only on exactly what you are doing in the present moment and nothing else.

Another example of a repetitive action that is good for

practicing mindfulness is doing a craft such as knitting. In order to knit something you must repeat stitch patterns over and over again. It is easy to let your mind drift when doing so (unless, of course, you are working with a difficult pattern). Practice mindfulness while knitting or doing any other repetitive activity by focusing solely on that activity.

Exercise no.	37 (3.19)
Goal	To use an everyday activity as a focus for concentration.
Minimum length of time	10 minutes
Location	anywhere
Needs	an activity
Steps	

1. Begin your meditation with your outer procedure steps 1-6.
2. Get into your sitting position.
3. Relax your body.
4. Begin a repetitive activity.
5. Concentrate fully on that activity.
6. Stay focused on the present moment and activity.
7. End your meditation using the outer procedure steps 8-13.

Exercise 3.20 – The Concentration Mantra

Doing any one of the previous concentration exercises will help you experience what it is like to have the mind fully engaged and focused. Recall those experiences and assign a word that will help you remember that sense of concentration. I will use the word *focus* but you should choose one that is best for you. When you say that word, let your mind become completely open and ready to maintain its focus on whatever you assign it. For this exercise, get into your relaxed sitting position and simply repeat your mental mantra as you concentrate your thoughts only on the present moment and the experience of repeating that mantra. If you drift off, slowly and gently bring yourself back to the mantra and begin again.

Chapter Three

Exercise no.	38 (3.20)
Goal	To assign a mantra to the experience of concentration.
Minimum length of time	10 minutes
Location	anywhere
Needs	none
Steps	

1. Begin your meditation with your outer procedure steps 1-6.
2. Get into your sitting position.
3. Relax your body.
4. Repeat your concentration mantra.
5. Recall the experience of complete concentration.
6. End your meditation using the outer procedure steps 8-13.

| Exercise 3.21 – The Concentration Mudra |

Choose a hand position to remind your mind and body of the experience of full concentration. I suggest that you put your hands together in front of your forehead with the index fingers pointing up. If you do this exercise for some time you may want to rest your head upon your thumbs and index fingers. Hold this position as you begin your meditation and return to the concentration mantra. Repeat the mantra as you hold the mudra in place. Whenever you feel your mind becoming scattered, use this mudra to focus your thoughts.

Exercise no.	39 (3.21)
Goal	To assign a hand position to the experience of concentration.
Minimum length of time	10 minutes
Location	anywhere
Needs	none
Steps	

1. Begin your meditation with your outer procedure steps 1-6.
2. Get into your sitting position.
3. Relax your body.
4. Form your concentration mudra.
5. Begin repeating your concentration mantra.
6. Recall the experience of complete concentration.
7. Continue for several minutes then end your meditation using the outer procedure steps 8-13.

Part Three – Acceptance

The work of Acceptance is a meditation of the heart. It calls you to learn to accept yourself, all others, and the world in which you live. It is not always an easy task as some people, unfortunately, are not taught how to appreciate their own natural worth. For many reasons, it is advantageous for others to try and make you feel less of yourself. That is how others gain power and influence over you. Through the practice of acceptance you can acknowledge or regain your sense of personal value. Your meditation should feel like a special time for you.

Chapter Three

It is a gift you give yourself. Allow it to be so by being comfortable with who you are and with the universe in which you live. Open up your heart to yourself, to all those you know, and to your place in the arms of Earth. Through these meditation exercises, allow your heart to become aware of your feelings and of the feelings of those around you. In our society, this type of practice is often frowned upon. If you find it difficult to do these exercises, I encourage you to let go of that curious need to live the image of the rough and tough person who never acknowledges nor shares any feelings. There may be times when such an attitude may be useful but I guarantee you that there will be times when it will be a great disadvantage to you. Let these exercises open that emotional part of you that needs to be recognized and expressed.

We will approach this area of the heart on three levels: the personal, the social, and the universal. On the personal level you are asked to accept yourself just for who you are at this point in time. We are all works in progress and we are all imperfect. Believe it or not, that is exactly how things are supposed to be. Come to accept your imperfections. You have skills and abilities that others do not (even if you have not found them yet). You also have inadequacies. Learn to accept and use both. On the social level, you are asked to accept all others for just who they are at this point in time. There will always be those to whom you feel a connection and there will always be those who will put you off. Just as you have skills, talents, curious quirks, and inadequacies, so do others and you can learn to accept them just as you have accepted yourself. On the universal level, you are asked to accept the world just as it is – all people, all places, and all parts of the universe.

Let me say that practicing acceptance is not the same as being acquiescent. Certainly there are serious challenges in the world and there may even be some in your own life. If you have the opportunity to do some good for yourself or have the chance to make the world a better more peaceful place then, by all means, I encourage you to do so, but the first step in making positive changes is to recognize the problem. You cannot fix a problem if you deny that it even exists in the first place. Acceptance is the opposite of denial. Through acceptance we recognize the current condition of something just as it is – blemishes and all. Only after accepting the situation can we then consider how to improve upon it. Being acquiescent means that you give into or ignore the challenges in your life and allow things to remain unchanged. Acceptance allows you to see something for what it is and then make plans for any necessary changes.

For many of the exercises in this section I will be encouraging you to use affirmations which are short positive statements you use to bolster your acceptance of things. It may feel a bit awkward to use these affirmations at first. They may seem too much like the quick fix affirmations offered in many pop psychology books. I do not believe that any of these affirmations will fix all of your life problems simply by repeating them but, if done seriously, they can increase your sense of acceptance. I hope you will try them out in a serious effort and, as always, feel free to change the words to make them work better for you.

Exercise 3.22 – Acceptance of the Self: Taking Inventory

In this exercise, you are asked to catalog your strengths and weaknesses. I firmly believe that everyone has both many strengths as well as weaknesses. I encourage you to list at least 20 strengths, 10 weaknesses, and 10 things that make you happy. If you find it easier to list weaknesses than strengths then you may be the kind of person who has been taught to have a low self-esteem. Take the opportunity to really dig deep and find those abilities that you have. It is not that some people have special abilities and some do not, some people have just not explored enough to find and develop those personal strengths. As a teacher, I have seen many people (through hard work and determination) find and develop their talents when they thought they had none. Take the time to explore things that interest you and then allow yourself to develop any ability you may have. You do not have to become an expert in whatever you do - just become good enough so that you enjoy that activity. Finding things you enjoy helps you learn about yourself and helps you to accept yourself for who you are.

Consider those things which are your strengths. Do not take into consideration *how* good you are; that is not relevant here. If you are even just a little good at something consider it a strength. Then consider your weaknesses but do it in a compassionate manner. Do not be harsh to yourself by placing a judgment value on the weakness - just recognize it for what it is. Next, consider those things that make you happy or bring you joy. If you have trouble finding strengths then think about those things that make you happy and consider ways in which you could pursue those interests in order to discover new strengths. When you are done with the meditation, write those things you considered into the following chart. Strive to fill it completely through subsequent meditations or through pursuing those interests.

	Personal Inventory		
	My Strengths	My Weaknesses	Things I Enjoy
1			
2			
4			
5			
6			
7			
8			
9			
10			

Just Being

Exercise no.	40 (3.22)
Goal	To take into account your strengths and weaknesses.
Minimum length of time	10 minutes
Location	anywhere
Needs	pen and paper
Steps	

1. Begin your meditation with your outer procedure steps 1-6.
2. Get into your sitting position.
3. Relax your body.
4. Focus your mind.
5. Consider those things which are your strengths.
6. Write them down.
7. Consider those things which are your weaknesses.
8. Write them down.
9. Consider those things which make you happy.
10. Write them down.
11. End your meditation using the outer procedure steps 8-13.

Exercise 3.23 – Acceptance of the Self: An Affirmation

For this exercise, begin in your relaxed meditation position and focus your mind. Memorize the following affirmation and then repeat it as you meditate. Allow the words to reach deep into yourself until you find it easy to accept yourself.

Chapter Three

Exercise no.	41 (3.23)
Goal	To become accepting of the self through an affirmation.
Minimum length of time	10 minutes
Location	anywhere
Needs	none
Steps	

1. Begin your meditation with your outer procedure steps 1-6.
2. Get into your sitting position.
3. Relax your body.
4. Focus your mind.
5. Repeat the Personal Affirmation for several minutes.
6. End your meditation with the outer procedure steps 8 - 13.

Personal Affirmation

I accept myself just as I am in this point in time
with all my strengths and weaknesses,
with all my joys and sorrows,
and with all my beauties and blemishes.
I understand that I am a work in progress –
that I can always strive to be better
but that I also have much to honor.
Let me find contentment in the present and hope for the future.

Illustration 19: Personal Affirmation

Exercise 3.24 – Acceptance of Others: Taking Inventory

Just as you did with yourself, I invite you to take stock of the people around you. Make a list of at least 10 people whose company you enjoy and 10 people who annoy you. For each, list the reasons for your selections. Unlike the previous listing, it is not important that you have an equal number in each category. In fact, as you learn to accept others, your list of those who annoy you will eventually diminish (if you even have one at all). It is important that you are honest with yourself. You do not have to share this information with anyone else so there is no advantage for you to be otherwise. Enter

Just Being

into your meditation position and focus your thoughts on those people with whom you associate on a daily basis. Consider each person and how you feel about him or her. When you have finished, fill in the charts below. Take note of the reasons you list in each chart and notice if there is anything you can learn about yourself and how you relate to other people. Try to find ways to learn to accept people just for who they are.

Just because you accept someone does not mean that you have to also be vulnerable. You can accept others for who they are and still insist on your own safety. Accepting a person is not the same as accepting that person's actions. Inflicting harm without due reason is wrong no matter who may do it. You can accept and respect yourself and others while still demanding that others do the same for you.

	Social Inventory 1	
	People Who I Enjoy	My Reasons
1		
2		
4		
5		
6		
7		
8		
9		
10		

| Social Inventory 2 ||
People Who Annoy Me	My Reasons
1	
2	
4	
5	
6	
7	
8	
9	
10	

Exercise no.	42 (3.24)
Goal	To take into account the people you know.
Minimum length of time	10 minutes
Location	anywhere
Needs	pen and paper
Steps	

1. Begin your meditation with your outer procedure steps 1-6.
2. Get into your sitting position.
3. Relax your body.
4. Focus your mind.
5. Consider those people you enjoy and why.
6. Make a list of those people.
7. Consider those people who annoy you and why.
8. Make a list of those people.
9. End your meditation with the outer procedure steps 8-13.

Exercise 3.25: Acceptance of Others: An Affirmation

Use the list you made in the last exercise to do this exercise. Think of those people as you repeat the affirmation below.

Exercise no.	43 (3.25)
Goal	To accept others.
Minimum length of time	10 minutes
Location	anywhere
Steps	

1. Begin your meditation with your outer procedure steps 1-6.
2. Get into your sitting position.
3. Relax your body.
4. Focus your mind.
5. Repeat your Social Affirmation for several minutes.
6. End your meditation with the outer procedure steps 8-13.

Social Affirmation

I accept others just as they are in this point in time
with all their strengths and weaknesses,
with all their joys and sorrows,
and with all their beauties and blemishes.
I understand that my relationships with others
is an ongoing process –
that I can always strive to be more compassionate
but that I also have much to offer.
Let me find peace in the presence of others.

Illustration 20: Social Affirmation

Exercise 3.26 – Accepting All: Taking Inventory

Accepting all means being tolerant of all things in the environment around you. There are some things you simply cannot change. Being mad at the weather make no sense and is a waste of precious life energy. You cannot change the weather no matter how hard you wish or how many spells you cast. The weather; sports scores; the presence of trees and mountains; annoying insects; the common cold; clouds and rain; disabilities; our hearts, minds, and bodies; other hearts, minds, and bodies; the universal needs of love, expression, and rest; and even life and death are all results of complex

Chapter Three

interactions of energies which follow the laws of physics just as you and I must do as well. As in the exercise with accepting others, come up with a list of things in the universe that cause you joy and things in the universe that annoy you. Your lists should include only things which are not directly caused by other people. As you become more tolerant of things, your list of joys should increase.

  Your challenge is to take those things that you list as annoyances and find a way to turn them into joyful activities or to make them into spiritual practices of tolerance and growth. You have heard of the phrase "turning lemons into lemonade." That is the goal here. Try to take those things which are sour and find a way to add a little sugar and water until they become something refreshing.

	Universal Inventory 1	
	Things which bring me joy	My Reasons
1		
2		
4		
5		
6		
7		
8		
9		
10		

Universal Inventory 2	
	Things which annoy me	My Reasons
1		
2		
4		
5		
6		
7		
8		
9		
10		

Exercise no.	44 (3.26)
Goal	To take into account all things.
Minimum length of time	10 minutes
Location	anywhere
Needs	pen and paper
Steps	

1. Begin your meditation with your outer procedure steps 1-6.
2. Get into your sitting position.
3. Relax your body.
4. Focus your mind.
5. Consider all the things you enjoy and why.
6. Write them down.
7. Consider all the things you do not enjoy and why.
8. Write them down.
9. End your meditation with the outer procedure steps 8-13.

Exercise 3.27 – Acceptance of All: An Affirmation

Consider all the things that you wrote down in the previous exercise. Use this exercise to meditate upon them using the affirmation below to work on learning to accept the world as it is.

Exercise no.	45 (3.27)
Goal	To accept all things.
Minimum length of time	10 minutes
Location	anywhere
Needs	none
Steps	

1. Begin your meditation with your outer procedure steps 1-6.
2. Get into your sitting position.
3. Relax your body.
4. Focus your mind.
5. Repeat the Universal Affirmation for several minutes.
6. End your meditation using the outer procedure steps 8-13.

Universal Affirmation

I accept all things just as they are in this point in time
with all their advantages and disadvantages.
Let me learn to become aware of the things I can change
and of the things that I cannot.
If I cannot change something,
let me learn to live with it.
I understand that my relationship with the world
is an ongoing process –
that I can always strive to be more accepting
but that I also have much to give.
Let me find joy in the complexities of the universe.

Illustration 21: A Universal Affirmation

Exercise 3.28 – Pagan Loving-Kindness

This exercise was inspired by a Buddhist loving-kindness meditation but has been adopted here into a Pagan version. Begin by getting into your relaxed sitting position and focusing on your mind. Begin to breathe deeply and fully. As you breathe, imagine that the pores of your body breathe in energy from Earth and from the space around you. Slowly fill yourself with this energy. This energy can have a sensation like warmth or an image like light or it may have a pleasant tingly feeling – whatever you may experience. It should be a pleasant sensation that is both relaxing and soothing. Continue to breathe in this energy and slowly allow it to fill a space around you. You can imagine a sphere or an egg-shaped area around your body that becomes filled with this energy. In effect, it becomes a very comforting cocoon of energy. As you do this, repeat the following affirmation.

> **Loving-Kindness Affirmation 1**
>
> May I be filled with this energy of life.
> May I be blessed by the spirit of love and compassion.
> Through it may I be healthy.
> Through it may I be wise.
> Through it may I be happy.
> Through it may I find peace.
> Through it may I be connected with myself.

Illustration 22: Loving-Kindness Affirmation I

Next, extend that energy outward into a much larger sphere. Bring into that sphere images of all the people you know and love. As you do so, repeat the next affirmation.

> **Loving-Kindness Affirmation 2**
>
> May those I love be filled with this energy of life.
> May they be blessed by the spirit of love and compassion.
> Through it may they be healthy.
> Through it may they be wise.
> Through it may they be happy.
> Through it may they find peace.
> Through it may we be connected.

Illustration 23: Loving-Kindness Affirmation II

The next step may be more challenging because it asks you to send the same energy of loving-kindness to all people regardless of whether or not you know them. You should include in this affirmation all the people you have ever known or met no matter how briefly. You should also include any who you do not like as well. This is a good practice for forgiveness. Allow your space of energy to become very large so that you can fit in all these people that you have encountered throughout your life. As you do so, repeat the next affirmation.

> **Loving-Kindness Affirmation 3**
>
> May all those I have known be filled with this energy of life.
> May they be blessed by the spirit of love and compassion.
> Through it may they be healthy.
> Through it may they be wise.
> Through it may they be happy.
> Through it may they find peace.
> Through it may we be connected.

Illustration 24: Loving-Kindness Affirmation III

The final step of the process asks you to accept the whole world just as it is in the same way that you learned to accept yourself and all others. This acceptance includes all the people you have never met, all creatures, and all parts of Earth and the universe. This is a large bill to fill and can only really be done in an abstract sense but it does teach you to be more accepting of the reality of the world as it is. It also means that you will need to accept the fact that bad things happen and that good things happen. The world is full of joy and pain. We can do our best to reduce pain and increase joy but we must realize that both will always be with us. To do this part of the exercise, continue to expand your sphere of energy and imagine that it slowly envelops the world. As you do so, repeat this affirmation:

Loving-Kindness Affirmation 4

May all beings be filled with this energy of life.
May they be blessed by the spirit of love and compassion.
Through it may all beings be healthy.
Through it may all beings be wise.
Through it may all beings be happy.
Through it may all beings find peace.
Through it may Earth be honored and healthy
Through it may all beings be connected-
to each other and to Earth.

Illustration 25: Loving-Kindness Affirmation IV

Exercise no.	46 (3.28)
Goal	To develop loving-kindness toward all beings.
Minimum length of time	10 minutes
Location	anywhere
Steps	

1. Begin your meditation with your outer procedure steps 1-6.
2. Get into your sitting position.
3. Relax your body.
4. Focus your mind.
5. Repeat the first Loving-kindness Affirmation for a few moments.
6. Become accepting of yourself.
7. Repeat the second Loving-kindness Affirmation for a few moments.
8. Become accepting of those you know and love.
9. Repeat the third Loving-kindness Affirmation for a few moments.
10. Become accepting of all others.
11. Repeat the fourth Loving-kindness Affirmation for a few moments.
12. Become accepting of the world.
13. End your meditation using the outer procedure steps 8-13.

Exercise 3.29 – The Acceptance Mantra

Find a word that will remind you of the feelings of complete acceptance that you discovered in the previous meditations. I will suggest the word "open" but you should choose the one that works best for you. When you repeat the word, let it automatically open your heart to be more accepting of yourself, others, and of the world.

Exercise no.	47 (3.29)
Goal	To attach a word to the experience of acceptance.
Minimum length of time	10 minutes
Location	anywhere
Needs	acceptance mantra
Steps	

1. Begin your meditation with your outer procedure steps 1-6.
2. Repeat your Acceptance Mantra in your mind.
3. Allow it to remind you of the experiences of acceptance you had in the previous exercises.
4. Continue for as long as you can.
5. End your meditation using the outer procedure steps 8-13.

Exercise 3.30 – The Acceptance Mudras

Find several hand motions, positions, or gestures that help to remind you of your feelings of acceptance you experienced on all three levels (yourself, others, and the world). I suggest that you do three positions that can be put together into one motion. I will offer my suggestions but you should find the ones that work best for you. To represent acceptance of the self, cross your arms over your chest in an "X" pattern. Your fingers should touch your shoulders. To represent acceptance of others, uncross your arms with hands palms up and bring them forward in front of your shoulders as if you were about to carry a load of wood in your arms. To represent acceptance of the world move your hands further out away from your shoulders as if you were about to give someone a big hug. For each position, you might say to yourself: "I am open to myself, I am open to others, I am open to the world." Then let your hands come into a relaxed position.

In later practices, you can simply repeat the mantra "open" as you turn the three positions into one graceful motion.

Exercise no.	48 (3.30)
Goal	To attach a hand position to the experience of acceptance.
Minimum length of time	10 minutes
Location	anywhere
Steps	

1. Begin your meditation with your outer procedure steps 1-6.
2. Sit in your meditation position
3. Relax your body
4. Focus your mind.
5. Cross your arms over your chest and say "I am open to myself."
6. Bring your hands out in front of your shoulders and say "I am open to others."
7. Bring your hands further out and say "I am open to the world."
8. Let your hands and arms relax.
9. Enjoy your feeling of total acceptance.
10. End your meditation with the outer procedure steps 8-13.

Part Four – Absorption

Absorption is the meditation of the soul – the part of the self most closely connected to Spirit. Your goal through absorption is to become completely united with the object or focus of your meditation until you become absorbed with it and there is no difference between you and it or, for that matter, between you and everything else. In the state of Absorption there is no sense of time and you either expand or diminish your sense of self until you become the world around you. Since all things possess the energy of Spirit, then merging with the environment is also a union with the divine.

Chapter Three

Exercise 3.31 – Slowing Time

This exercise is meant to let you have an experience of slowing down time. Whether or not time actually changes during your meditation will be for you to determine. Modern physics teaches us that time is relative although we experience it as a constant in our daily lives. In reality, time is directly related to the gravitational mass of a particular object like Earth but is not universally constant. Before you begin your meditation take a note of the time you start and end it and notice if that reality is different than your experience of time during the meditation. We will use counting and the breath as a means of experiencing time differently.

Exercise no.	49 (3.31)
Goal	To experience to sensation of slowing down time.
Minimum length of time	10 minutes
Location	anywhere
Steps	

1. Begin your meditation with your outer procedure steps 1-6.
2. Sit in your meditation position
3. Relax your body
4. Focus your mind.
5. Be open to yourself, all others, and the world.
6. Count backwards from 30 in an approximate speed of one count per second. Breathe normally.
7. Count backwards from 30 at approximately half the speed as before. Breathe half as slow.
8. Again, count backwards from 30 at approximately half the speed as before. Breathe half as slow.
9. And yet once more, count backwards from 30 at approximately half the speed as before. Breathe half as slow.
10. Breathe very slowly. At the end of the inhalation, hold your breathe and experience the sensation of time stopping completely. Do this for 30 counts and then gradually return your breath to normal.
11. End you meditation using the outer procedure steps 8-13.

Exercise 3.32 – Self Expansion

This exercise is similar to the expanding sphere you experienced in the Acceptance meditations except that you will work on expanding yourself rather than just an energy form. You will need your imagination and a willingness to let go of physical realities. You will need to be able to see yourself as much larger than you are. Once again, I will refer to that old classic horror movie *The Blob*. This alien creature resembled nothing more than a ball of jelly and began at about the size of a baseball but as it consumed more and more, it grew in greater proportions until it became large enough to engulf whole houses. You will be asked to see yourself in the same way but in a less destructive manner. In another example, there was an episode of the original *Star Trek* (Am I showing my age yet?) in which a living being existed in the form of a ring of energy that could envelop a human and, by doing so, communicate with it *(The Metamorphosis*, Season 2 Episode 9). This is closer to the image you will want to create in your mind. Allow yourself to become a being of pure energy that can eventually expand - but as you do so, become part of that which you surround so that the energies of yourself and the energies of that which is around you intermingle until you become one and the same.

Exercise no.	50 (3.32)
Goal	To experience a sense of expanding the self.
Minimum length of time	10 minutes
Location	anywhere
Steps	

1. Begin your meditation with your outer procedure steps 1-6.
2. Sit in your meditation position
3. Relax your body
4. Focus your mind.
5. Be open to yourself, all others, and the world.
6. In your mind, change your image of yourself from a human form into a sphere of pure energy.
7. Feel that energy swirl and move.
8. Take a deep breath. Then let out a long exhalation that serves to expand your sphere of energy until it is about a foot larger.
9. Breathe normally and feel your energy swirl within that space.
10. After a few moments, take another large breath and exhale your energy until you envelop the entire room you are in.
11. Breathe normally and feel your energy mingling with all the objects in the room. Experience yourself actually becoming each object until you and everything else become connected as one swirling sphere of energy.
12. Take another deep breath and exhale your energy until you envelop your entire living space.
13. Breathe normally and, once again, become each object you encounter and envelop.
14. Continue this process for as far as you can. Each time you practice this exercise, try to expand even further until you can envelope the entire world.
15. End your meditation using the outer procedure steps 8-13

Exercise 3.33 – Self Dissolution

This exercise will approach Absorption through the exact opposite process of the previous exercise. At first this may seem odd but both exercises are meant to reach the same goal. If you understand the concept that all things flow in circles and cycles then the concept may not seem so odd. It is a law of nature that at the end of any extreme is the opposite of that extreme. At the end of complete expansion or complete dissolution is the same experience of

Absorption. In this exercise, you will shrink yourself and if you need a movie reference then think about *Honey, I Shrunk The Kids*.

Exercise no.	51 (3.33)
Goal	To experience a sense of shrinking the self.
Minimum length of time	10 minutes
Location	anywhere
Steps	

1. Begin your meditation with your outer procedure steps 1-6.
2. Sit in your meditation position
3. Relax your body
4. Focus your mind.
5. Be open to yourself, all others, and the world.
6. In your mind change yourself from a human to a sphere of pure energy.
7. Take a deep breath and as you slowly breathe out let that energy reduce in size until the objects around you in your mind become enormous in size.
8. Breathe normally and experience yourself in this form.
9. After a few moments, take another deep breath and exhale yourself into an even smaller form that can intermingle with cellular objects.
10. Breathe normally and experience yourself in this form.
11. After a few moments, take another deep breath and exhale yourself into a form small enough to interact at the atomic level.
12. Breathe normally and experience yourself at this level.
13. After a few moments, take yet another deep breath and exhale yourself until you become pure quantum energy and connect with all things.
14. Breathe normally and experience yourself at this level.
15. After a few moments, expand yourself slowly until you have reached your normal size.
16. End your meditation using the outer procedure steps 8-13.

Chapter Three

Exercise 3.34 – Entering Flow

Unlike most of the previous experiences, this one is an active meditation. With it, you experience Absorption by becoming totally connected to an activity. The activity can be almost anything but a very repetitive action works well. For me, writing is an active meditation. There is the constant tapping on the computer keyboard and I become completely absorbed with the subject matter about which I am writing. The activity can be something much simpler than writing a book, however. Many people feel a sense of absorption in sports activities like running or in hobbies like knitting or gardening or it can even be practiced in mundane activities that might otherwise be considered boring. Such activities may include washing the dishes or painting the house. The important thing is to enter into the activity so completely that you become completely absorbed with it. In such a state, you may experience a different sense of time and space as you become completely lost in the present moment.

Exercise no.	52 (3.34)
Goal	To experience a sense of flow.
Minimum length of time	10 minutes
Location	anywhere
Needs	a repetitive activity
Steps	

1. Begin your meditation with your outer procedure steps 1-6.
2. Sit in your meditation position
3. Relax your body
4. Focus your mind.
5. Be open to yourself, all others, and the world.
6. Begin a repetitive motion or activity.
7. Breathe into the motions of that activity.
8. Concentrate all your thoughts on the motions of that activity.
9. Continue for as long as you engage in that activity.
10. End your meditation using the outer procedure steps 8-13.

Exercise 3.35 – The Absorption Mantra

Find a word that helps to remind yourself of the things you just experienced with the previous Absorption exercises. I will suggest the use of the word "connect" but use whatever word works best for you. Repeat the word several times in your mind as you do the meditation and recall your sense of feeling connected to all things.

Exercise no.	53 (3.35)
Goal	To attach a word to the experience of absorption.
Minimum length of time	10 minutes
Location	anywhere
Needs	an absorption mantra
Steps	

1. Begin your meditation with your outer procedure steps 1-6.
2. Sit in your meditation position
3. Relax your body
4. Focus your mind.
5. Be open to yourself, all others, and the world.
6. Begin repeating your absorption mantra.
7. Choose a focus for your meditation.
8. Slow your breath and feel time begin to slow.
9. Either expand or diminish yourself until you and the object of focus are united.
10. Remain in unity with the object for as long as you can.
11. Return to your original self.
12. End your meditation using the outer procedure steps 8-13.

Exercise 3.36 – The Absorption Mudra

Find a hand position that will remind your body of your experiences of Absorption. I suggest putting your hands together in front of you with fingertips touching and thumbs interlaced. This is similar to a prayer position for many traditions. With your hands connected to each other and your thumbs intertwined you have a physical reminder of connecting two things together. Though your hands cannot physically absorb each other, the energy of each hand can be absorbed into one small sphere of energy that will exist within your palms thus clearly symbolizing your goal.

Exercise no.	54 (3.36)
Goal	To attach a hand position to the experience of absorption.
Minimum length of time	10 minutes
Location	anywhere
Needs	an absorption mudra
Steps	

1. Begin your meditation with your outer procedure steps 1-6.
2. Sit in your meditation position
3. Relax your body
4. Focus your mind.
5. Be open to yourself, all others, and the world.
6. Bring your hands together in front of you with fingertips touching and thumbs interlaced.
7. Slow your breath and feel time begin to slow.
8. Diminish yourself into the sphere of energy between your palms.
9. Become united with that energy.
10. Return to your original self.
11. End your meditation using the outer procedure steps 8-13.

Part Five – Combined Procedure

You have spent a good deal of time learning to experience complete relaxation, to focus your mind in concentration, to be accepting of yourself and all others and to absorb yourself completely into your meditation. Through these exercises you have learned to prepare and engage your body, mind, heart, and soul into your practice. In this section, we will put together all those experiences into one single practice so that you can continue on to deeper meditations.

Exercise 3.37 – The Combined Inner Procedure

This exercise combines all the previous exercises into one.

Exercise no.	55 (3.37)
Goal	To create an inner meditation procedure.
Minimum length of time	5 minutes
Location	anywhere
Needs	none
Steps	

1. Begin your meditation with your outer procedure steps 1-6.
2. Get into your sitting position.
3. Form the relaxation mudra and repeat the relaxation mantra in your mind.
4. Recall the experience of being completely relaxed.
5. Move into the concentration mudra and repeat the concentration mudra in your mind.
6. Recall the experience of focusing your mind.
7. Move into the three acceptance mudras and repeat the acceptance mantra in your mind.
8. Recall the experience of accepting yourself, all others, and Earth.
9. Move into the absorption mudra and repeat the absorption mantra in your mind.
10. Recall the experience of becoming completely absorbed.
11. Let your hands relax gently in your lap or on your knees.
12. Sit quietly for a few moments and enjoy the experience.
13. End you meditation using the outer procedure steps 8-13.

Exercise 3.38 – The Combined Outer and Inner Procedures

This exercise combines both the Inner and Outer Procedure to become one procedure. Strive to create a simple and short routine that will bring you instantly into a meditative state of mind and prepare you for your chosen meditative work. By this point in your practice, the Outer Procedure should be short and refined. The Inner Procedure should become a simple flowing motion incorporating all of your mudras into one while using the four mantras to remind yourself of your earlier practices. The mudras I have chosen in this chapter can be put together into one seamless motion but, as always, you should feel free to create a pattern that is most comfortable to you.

Exercise no.	56 (3.38)
Goal	To create an unified meditation procedure.
Minimum length of time	strive to get it down to 2 minutes or less
Location	anywhere
Needs	none
Steps	

1. Begin your meditation with your outer procedure steps 1-6.
2. Get into your sitting position.
3. Do all the mudras as one continuous motion. As you pass through each mudra, say the mantra associated with it.
4. Sit quietly for a few moments.
5. End you meditation using the outer procedure steps 8-13.

Just Being

Chapter Four

Chapter Four

Pagan Meditations

Introduction

The purpose of this chapter is to offer meditations that are specifically designed for Pagan spiritual practice. Spiritual meditations often have certain requirements that are in addition to other meditations. They may involve connection with a deity or spiritual principle. Spiritual meditation practice needs to reflect the particular theology being expressed or explored in the meditation. This may include the use of specific symbols or ritual practices. Pagan meditations can work to connect the practitioner to the energy of all life – Spirit. It may reflect a desire to seek this inner Spirit through exploration of the mysterious. Divination and occult studies are some ways to explore the mysteries of the universe. Divination, when used as a method to communicate with the divine within and beyond each of us, often has a close relationship to meditation. Divinatory symbols or uniquely Pagan symbols such as the pentagram or the elements can be used as centers of focus. Each of these methods of Pagan meditation will be explored here.

For each of the meditations in this chapter, I will assume that you have developed your Outer and Inner Procedures and that you can do them both quickly and easily as one combined procedure. At this point, the combined procedure should only take a few moments of your time and should come freely and naturally. You can, of course, skip all the preparatory meditations and the procedures of the preceding chapters and can get much from the meditations in this chapter alone but it is my experience that your meditations will be deeper and more fulfilling if you can prepare yourself beforehand.

The following meditations are divided into four large categories relating to the four parts of the self. Meditations are classified as either physical, mental, emotional, or spiritual. These categories are arbitrary. They reflect what the primary purpose of the meditation may be but all the meditations will involve all parts of the self to some degree or another. Each is designed to be done as a guided meditation in which you guide yourself by memorizing the steps and leading yourself or by recording the steps and playing them back later. They can also be done in a group meditation with one person reading the steps while others practice the meditation.

This chapter also includes an example of an open meditation. This type of meditation has no focus at all and can be quite challenging. Though an open meditation is, by definition, not a specifically Pagan form of meditation, if the meditator is Pagan then the open meditation will reflect the presence of the person doing it.

Exercises

Part One – Physical Meditations

The meditations in this section involve primarily using the body to become involved in your meditation. We will look at two major ways in which this can be done. The first will be using arts and crafts as the meditative focus and the second section will focus on using the physical body itself and the body's senses. The arts and crafts meditations will focus on those things that most people can do. Though I firmly believe that all people are capable of some artistic ability, few have the ability to do all. For example, though I enjoy creating and performing music and I also like to write, my drawing ability has always been limited. I will focus on those things that do not require a specific artistic ability like being able to play an instrument or knowing how to paint a portrait. If you have a special artistic ability then I hope these exercises will inspire you to find a way to connect your art to your spiritual practice.

Exercise 4.1 – Making Pagan Prayer Beads

The next two exercises involve activities which both can be used as a meditation. The first activity is to create a prayer bead chain and the second uses the prayer beads as a means for focusing a meditation. To make a prayer bead chain, first collect together your materials. Choose whatever objects that best reflect your practice and your preferences. To make one similar to one I have made and used, you will need the following materials: 8 oblong shaped connector beads; 5 white, 5 gold (or yellow), and 5 black (or dark) round beads; 13 very small spacer beads (I used silver ones); 1 square bead; 1 small pentagram pendant; 1 hook or latch; and some material for stringing all these together (I used hemp). A symbol for each and the construction of the chain is illustrated below.

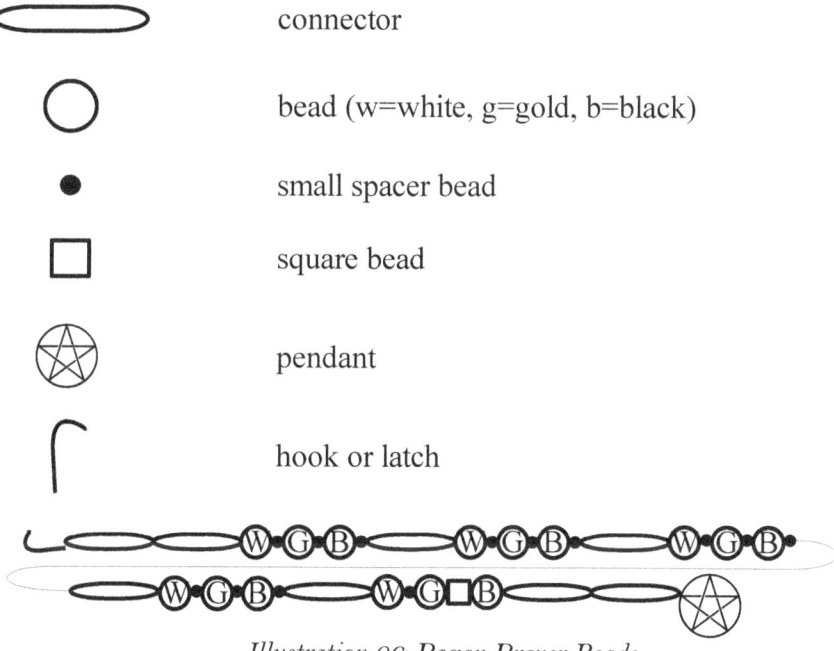

Illustration 26: Pagan Prayer Beads

Each of the beads has significance in relation to my Pagan spiritual path. The 8 long connector beads relate to the eight Sabbats. The 13 small silver spacers represent the 13 moons in a year. The 3 colors of the main beads represent the forces of Light, Love, and Life and the 3 celestial bodies: yellow for the sun, white for the moon, and black for the stars. They are repeated five times to represent the five precepts of my practice: Reason, Respect, Responsibility, Reverence, and Revelry. The square bead at the end stands for the four elements and is also used as a reminder that the chain is ending. I used wooden beads and hemp because both are strong materials representative of

Earth. The pentagram at the end represents Paganism and the four elements plus Spirit.

Chapter Four

Exercise no.	57 (4.1)
Goal	To make a Pagan prayer bead chain.
Minimum length of time	20 minutes
Location	anywhere
Needs	a variety of beads and some string (see above)
Steps	

1. Do your outer and inner meditation procedures.
2. Begin making your prayer bead chain. As you place each item on your chain contemplate upon what it means to you in your practice. In this way, you will be placing the energy and intent of the meaning of each item into that item as you go. For example, if you were creating the chain illustrated above you might say the following as you place each bead (starting backward from the end):
   1. I place this pentagram to represent the four elements and Spirit.
   2. I place this bead (connector) to represent the Sabbat of Samhain: the height of Fall and the end of the Pagan year.
   3. I place this bead (connector) to represent the Sabbat of Mabon: the beginning of Fall.
   4. I place this bead (black bead) to represent the Dark Moon and the force of Life.
   5. I place this bead (square bead) to represent the four elements.
   6. I place this bead (gold bead) to represent the Sun and the force of Light.
   7. I place this bead (silver spacer) to represent the Esbat and my ritual practice.
   8. I place this bead (white bead) to represent the Full Moon and the force of Love which I honor through my vow of Revelry.
   9. I place this bead (connector) to represent the Sabbat of Lammas or the height of Summer.
   10. I place this bead (silver spacer) to represent the Esbat and my ritual practice.
   11. I place this bead (black bead) to represent the Dark Moon and the force of Life.
   12. I place this bead (silver spacer) to represent the Esbat and my ritual practice.

13. I place this bead (gold bead) to represent the Sun and the God of Light whom I honor through my vow of Reverence.
14. I place this bead (silver spacer) to represent the Esbat and my ritual practice.
15. I place this bead (white bead) to represent the Full Moon and the Goddess of Love whom I honor through my vow of Reverence.
16. I place this bead (connector) to represent the Sabbat of Litha or the beginning of Summer.
17. I place this bead (silver spacer) to represent the Esbat and my ritual practice.
18. I place this bead (black bead) to represent the Dark Moon and the Child of Life whom I honor through my vow of Responsibility.
19. I place this bead (silver spacer) to represent the Esbat and my ritual practice.
20. I place this bead (gold bead) to represent the Sun and the God of Light whom I honor through my vow of Responsibility.
21. I place this bead (silver spacer) to represent the Esbat and my ritual practice.
22. I place this bead (white bead) to represent the Full Moon and the Goddess of Love whom I honor through my vow of Responsibility.
23. I place this bead (connector) to represent the Sabbat of Beltane or the height of Spring.
24. I place this bead (silver spacer) to represent the Esbat and my ritual practice.
25. I place this bead (black bead) to represent the Dark Moon and the Child of Life whom I honor through my vow of Respect.
26. I place this bead (silver spacer) to represent the Esbat and my ritual practice.
27. I place this bead (gold bead) to represent the Sun and the God of Light whom I honor through my vow of Respect.
28. I place this bead (silver spacer) to represent the Esbat and my ritual practice.
29. I place this bead (white bead) to represent the Full Moon and the Goddess of Love whom I honor through my vow of Respect.
30. I place this bead (connector) to represent the Sabbat of Ostara or the beginning of Spring.
31. I place this bead (silver spacer) to represent the Esbat and

Chapter Four

      my ritual practice.
- 32. I place this bead (black bead) to represent the Dark Moon and the Child of Life whom I honor through my vow of Reason.
- 33. I place this bead (silver spacer) to represent the Esbat and my ritual practice.
- 34. I place this bead (gold bead) to represent the Sun and the God of Light whom I honor through my vow of Reason.
- 35. I place this bead (silver spacer) to represent the Esbat and my ritual practice.
- 36. I place this bead (white bead) to represent the Full Moon and the Goddess of Love whom I honor through my vow of Reason.
- 37. I place this bead (connector) to represent the Sabbat of Imbolc or the height of Winter.
- 38. I place this bead (connector) to represent the Sabbat of Yule or the beginning of Winter.
3. Add your hook and tie off your Prayer Bead chain.
4. End your meditation.

Exercise 4.2 – Using Pagan Prayer Beads

To use the prayer chain, you can work the beads between your thumb and forefinger. With each main bead, repeat mentally one of three lines of a mantra. Using the chain created above, for example, one mantra in three parts is repeated using each one of the sets of round beads. Each mantra is repeated five times. On the final mantra, the fingers reach the square bead and that is the signal that one set has been completed. Flip the chain and begin again. (Or if your chain is connected together like a necklace simply continue). I use a three part mantra such as "as within, so with all, so mote it be." In addition to the mantra itself, I use sets of five mantras (one length of the prayer chain) as a meditation. For the first three sets I concentrate on relaxing and calming the self. During the second set I focus on raising positive energy through my breath and on the third set I feel myself sending this positive energy out to all around me.

Exercise no.	58 (4.2)
Goal	Use your Pagan prayer bead chain.
Minimum length of time	20 minutes
Location	anywhere
Needs	your prayer beads
Steps	

1. Do your outer and inner meditation procedures.
2. Hold your your Prayer Bead chain in your hand at the hook.
3. Choose a mantra to use.
4. Work the chain in your hand until you feel the first bead with your fingers.
5. Begin your mantra and coordinate each part with a bead that you work between your fingers.
6. When you feel the square bead, you will know it is time to complete your mantra with the final bead in the chain.
7. Flip the chain over and begin again.
8. Continue for as long as you can.
9. End your meditation.

Chapter Four

Exercise 4.3 – Making a Meditation Shawl

You can, of course, use the making of any art or craft project into an active meditation. I will use here the example of a meditation shawl (sometimes called a prayer shawl) which is a work of crafted material about a foot or more in width and which reaches the length of your outstretched arms (around five feet). The shawl can be made through sewing, knitting, crochet, or macramé. A meditation shawl can be used as a gift for young mothers or people who are sick or distressed or can be given to people who want to use it during prayers or meditation. Of course, you can also make one for yourself and use it to bless your work as well as keep you warm during your practice. One advantage to making a shawl is that they are fairly easy to do. Most often they involve using a simple repeated pattern which, in itself, is conducive to meditation. You can make the shawl Pagan by adding symbols or designs to it and by blessing it when you are finished making it.

Exercise no.	59 (4.3)
Goal	To make a meditation shawl.
Minimum length of time	20 minutes
Location	anywhere
Needs	yarn and a pattern
Steps	

1. Find a pattern for making a meditation shawl.
2. Do your outer and inner meditation procedures.
3. Make the shawl using each row as a set for meditation.
4. Complete the shawl.
5. End your meditation.

Exercise 4.4 - Using a Meditation Shawl

When going into a meditation practice, it is helpful to do things to remind your body, mind, heart, and soul that it is time to enter into a different state of consciousness. The Outer and Inner Procedures with their mantras and mudras and your meditative sitting position are all meant to do just that. Sometimes is also helpful to use special clothing or materials as well. You may choose to use a special pillow (which could be yet another arts and crafts project) or you may choose to wear special clothing. For example, you may want to wear a special robe or cape or you may just want to don yourself with a prayer shawl. I suggest that you have something that is worn only when you meditate just for such a purpose and a shawl is a simple item that can be used. Do a meditation to bless your shawl and then use it each time you meditate.

Exercise no.	60 (4.4)
Goal	To use the meditation shawl.
Minimum length of time	20 minutes
Location	anywhere
Needs	your meditation shawl
Steps	

1. Do your outer and inner meditation procedures.
2. Put on your meditation shawl.
3. Do a simple meditation such as the repetition of a mantra like:
    "I wrap this shawl about me as the universe wraps its arms around me in love.
    It is an expression of my practice as I am an expression of the divine.
    It is the yolk that holds me in this timeless blessing of peace."
4. End your meditation.

Chapter Four

Exercise 4.5 – Chanting

Chanting is another good way to involve your body in meditation. As you practiced doing the "om" chant earlier you may have felt the vibration throughout your whole body. With chanting you can actually set in motion many vibrations at once - especially if you do it slowly. It helps to choose a chant that is easy and meaningful to you. Learn an easy chant or recall one that you may have learned and use that chant in this practice. The following is an example of a simple chant you can use.

Meditation Chant

As a-bove, so be-low. As with-in, so with all. bo-dy, mind, and heart en-thrall.

Illustration 27: A Meditation Chant

Exercise no.	61 (4.5)
Goal	To use a chant as a focus for meditation.
Minimum length of time	20 minutes
Location	anywhere
Needs	a chant to sing
Steps	

1. Begin your inner and outer procedures.
2. Begin your chant.
3. Repeat the chanting for as long as you can.
4. End your meditation.

Exercise 4.6 – Sacred Dancing

Sacred dancing is different than social dancing in that you are trying to connect with cosmic energies rather than just dancing for fun with other people. In our society, people are often discouraged from expressing themselves physically. If this is true for you then you may find this practice to be a challenge but it may also be just the thing you need. Free physical expression is, well, freeing. If you feel locked up in your own body or if you feel a sense of unbridled energy within you that never seems to get expressed, then a physical release such as the kind that you get from moving and dancing can be very joyful and invigorating. Find some music that is energetic and uplifting. It should have a strong driving rhythm but does not necessarily have to be very loud and fast. Choose your music carefully to find something that encourages movement but also helps you to focus on meditation. Try something exotic like Turkish Whirling Dervish music which is designed for a moving meditation. As you listen and move to the sounds, focus your thoughts entirely on the music itself. Forget completely that you are moving. Abstain from all judgments about how you may appear. Find a time and place when you can be completely undisturbed and free in your movements and expression.

Exercise no.	62 (4.6)
Goal	To use dancing as a focus for meditation.
Minimum length of time	20 minutes
Location	anywhere
Needs	music and something to play it on
Steps	

1. Do your inner and outer meditation procedures but remain standing.
2. Start the music and focus on your breath.
3. Let the music and its rhythms enter into your body through your breathe.
4. Do not think about moving. Rather, let motions simply happen on their own.
5. Continue moving throughout the music.
6. When the music ends, end your meditation.

Exercise 4.7 – Sacred Drumming

Playing a drum is something that anyone can do. Of course, you can take lessons to learn how to play a drum like a professional musician but lessons are not needed to make basic drum noises. Just rap on the drum head and you are making music. Playing the drum is a long standing meditative and spiritual practice; it is an essential practice of many shamans. You can actually alter your heart and brain wave patterns with drum beat patterns. For this exercise, however, I suggest that you keep it simple – especially if you have never drummed before. Begin by getting into a quiet space and beat a simple and continuous beat similar to your heart beat. You need do nothing else to drum as a meditation. If you begin to add other patterns or rhythms, that is fine but it is not necessary. Release all judgments about how or what you are doing. Just drum and keep drumming for as long as you can.

Exercise no.	63 (4.7)
Goal	To use drumming as a focus for meditation.
Minimum length of time	20 minutes
Location	anywhere
Needs	a drum
Steps	

1. Begin your outer and inner meditation procedures.
2. Begin drumming softly on your drum.
3. Focus on the rhythm and not on making the rhythm.
4. Let spontaneity guide you.
5. Continue drumming for as long as you can.
6. End your meditation.

Exercise 4.8 – Creating Your Own Mandala

In the previous chapter, we discussed the use of a mandala as a focus for your meditation. Sometimes the most powerful mandala is one that you make yourself. Mandalas are not difficult and can be as complex or as simple as you want them to be. Many mandalas are simply repeated geometric patterns so if you can draw or outline a simple shape you can create a mandala. You can draw it freehand or use a computer or cut out small triangles, circles, squares, or other shapes and use them as pattern guides. There are even web pages that help you create original mandalas. The essential elements for any mandala is that it be enclosed in a circle and that it should draw your attention into the center of the circle.

Exercise no.	64 (4.8)
Goal	To create a personal mandala.
Minimum length of time	20 minutes
Location	anywhere
Needs	drawing and art materials
Steps	

1. Gather together your materials you will use to make your mandala.
2. Begin your outer and inner meditation procedures.
3. Take a few moments to close your eyes and imagine a simple mandala.
4. Begin making your mandala by drawing a large circle.
5. With simple shapes and designs create your mandala.
6. Use the shapes to draw your attention to the center of the circle.
7. When done, spend a few moments looking at the mandala as a meditative focus.
8. End your meditation.

Chapter Four

Exercise 4.9 – The Pentagram Walk

One powerful way of doing an active meditation is through walking. In a basic walking meditation, you practice walking very slowly with your hands held loosely in front or behind you. As you walk, breathe slowly and fully and connect your breath with your steps. Your focus would be on feeling and enjoying the sensation of just walking quietly and with intent. I have added to this practice by developing a walking meditation done in the shape of a pentagram. To do a pentagram walk, you will need a large open space and some flag markers that can be purchased at any hardware store. Identify the space you will use by imagining a circle. Go to the center of that circle. Imagine a pentagram shape etched onto the surface of your space. Mark each of the five points of the pentagram within the circle with five of the flags. You may begin your walking meditation by first circling the pentagram or by just starting at the top point of the pentagram and walking to each point until you return to the top. Choose a mantra or a focus for your meditation. The mantra below can be used as you walk. The letters "L" and "R" stand for the left foot and right foot and indicate how you can connect the mantra to your steps as you go. Remember to connect your breathing with your walking as well.

Walking Mantra

L　　R　　L　　R
Love and Light, Blessings Bright
L　　R　　L　　R
Let my path be true and right

Illustration 28: Walking Meditation Mantra

Exercise no.	65 (4.9)
Goal	To practice a form of walking meditation following the outline of a pentagram.
Minimum length of time	20 minutes
Location	on large open space
Needs	markers or flags
Steps	

1. Do your outer and inner meditation procedures.
2. Beginning at the top point of the pentagram, walk slowly and with intent to the next point on the pentagram indicated by the flag. As you step use your mantra to coordinate your thoughts and your steps. (If you want a longer walk then walk the circle around the pentagram first and then enter at the top.)
3. Do the same for each point on the pentagram.
4. When you reach the top point again, end your meditation.

Exercise 4.10 – The Cakes and Tea Ceremony

To involve the body fully in a meditation it is necessary to engage all the senses. In the following exercise, I have adopted a Cakes and Ale ceremony with a tea ceremony and made it into a Pagan Cakes and Tea Ceremony. The exercise here is designed for one person but I have included a version of the ceremony for a group in the Appendices. In this ceremony, all five senses are given attention. The sense of taste is heightened through the tea and some food. The tea, flowers, and the scented candle reach the sense of smell. The cups and a warm face cloth appeal to the sense of touch. The table setting and a bit of art on the table appeal to the sight while soft music is for the sense of hearing. To do the ceremony for one you will need a teapot or pot of hot water, a tea bag in your choice of flavor, a teacup, a chalice, a small plate with a treat such as a cookie, a face cloth in a large bowl, and a music player with some relaxing music in it.

Exercise no.	66 (4.10)
Goal	To access all the senses through a Pagan Cakes and Tea Ceremony.
Minimum length of time	20 minutes
Location	a large enough space to accommodate all the materials
Needs	tea, finger food, flowers, scented candle, teacups and saucers, face cloth, a small work of art, soft music and a player, teapot, tea bag, chalice, and a small plate.
Steps	

1. Do your outer and inner meditation procedures.
2. Begin the music.
3. Light a candle of intent.
4. Take a moment to center yourself.
5. Pour some warm water into the large bowl with the face cloth in it (a fragrant oil may be added).
6. Wash your hands and face while you repeat the mantra: "May all those whose lives I touch be blessed."
7. Place your chosen tea bag into the teacup and fill it with water.
8. Raise your cup and say "I bless this water with the flowers of the Earth. Let it nourish my body, my mind, my heart, and my soul."
9. Take the chalice in your left hand and raise your teacup in your right hand and say "From Earth I receive, to Earth I return." Pour a very small amount of tea into the chalice.
10. Put the chalice down while still holding the tea and say "May I receive this gift of the Earth with gratitude and may I return that gratitude through my good works."
11. Slowly drink the tea while repeating the mantra "May I be nourished."
12. Hold up the plate with the food and say "May I be thankful for this time."
13. Slowly eat the treat while repeating the mantra "May I be nourished."
14. End your meditation.

Just Being

Part Two – Mental Meditations

The meditations in this section involve using the mind as a focus. Symbols are a great way to stimulate contemplation since symbols can have layered meanings and significance. Tools of divination work well for symbolic contemplation since they often use spiritual symbolism. Tarot cards, rune stones, and even ordinary numbers can have layers of symbolic meaning.

Exercise 4.11 – Contemplation on the Pentagram

One of the most recognized Pagan symbols, the pentagram, can be a very powerful tool for contemplation. It is a simple design – a five pointed star set in a circle - but it can have many layers of meaning. Before you begin any symbolic meditation, however, it is important that you study about the symbol itself. Find as many sources on the meaning of the pentagram as you can. Like all symbols, the pentagram can mean many different things to different people. Of course, you can always affix to any symbol your own personal interpretations.

Exercise no.	67 (4.11)
Goal	To use a pentagram as a focus for contemplation.
Minimum length of time	20 minutes
Location	anywhere
Needs	a pentagram or other significant symbol
Steps	

1. Do your outer and inner meditation procedures.
2. Place a pentagram before you and begin focusing upon it.
3. Contemplate on all the meanings you have learned about it.
4. Seek your own meanings for the symbol.
5. Let your mind freely explore meanings, connections, and relationships.
6. End your meditation.

Chapter Four

Exercise 4.12 – A Pagan Mandala

In previous chapters you have practiced using a mandala and you have even made one of your own. In this exercise you will be asked to use a specifically Pagan mandala that I designed. As you have done before, let your mind be pulled into the many images and relationships that may be found within the design. Search for meaning in symbols and connections.

Exercise no.	68 (4.12)
Goal	To use a mandala with Pagan symbolism as a focus for contemplation.
Minimum length of time	20 minutes
Location	anywhere
Needs	a Pagan mandala
Steps	

1. Do your outer and inner meditation procedures.
2. Place the mandala in front of you and open your mind.
3. Contemplate the symbols and inter-relationships of the images.
4. Allow your mind to be drawn towards the center and be pulled into the mandala.
5. Continue for as long as you can.
6. End your meditation.

Just Being

Illustration 29: A Pagan Mandala

Chapter Four

Exercise 4.13 – Single Tarot Card Contemplation

Tarot cards are rich in symbolism and those images can be quite useful when doing a contemplative meditation. If you do not already have a Tarot deck but want to do this exercise then obtain one. Make sure you take your time looking for one that is best for you. Study the symbols and images. If those images speak to you then they will be useful to you. Read through the book that came with the cards and see what its creator's intent was but do not be tied to only that interpretation. You are free to find your own meanings and associations. In this exercise, you will be asked to simply choose or pick randomly one of the cards from the deck and then contemplate upon it.

Exercise no.	69 (4.13)
Goal	To use the symbolism on a Tarot card as a focus for contemplation.
Minimum length of time	20 minutes
Location	anywhere
Needs	a single Tarot card
Steps	

1. Do your outer and inner meditation procedures.
2. Choose a Tarot card from your deck.
3. Contemplate upon all the images and symbols on the card.
4. End your meditation.

Exercise 4.14 – Multiple Tarot Card Contemplation

This exercise expands upon the last by using three cards instead of just one. Using more than one card not only allows for more symbols to be contemplated, it also allows the cards to create a story through a spread. The position of the three cards becomes equally important to the symbols on the cards.

Exercise no.	70 (4.14)
Goal	To use a 3 card Tarot spread as a focus for contemplation.
Minimum length of time	20 minutes
Location	anywhere
Needs	3 Tarot cards
Steps	

1. Do your outer and inner meditation procedures.
2. Choose three cards from your deck and lay them in front of you, face up.
3. Place them so that they are next to each other.
4. Contemplate upon the symbols of the cards but also allow the cards to create a story such that the card on the left describes events in the past that have led to the card in the middle (the present) and that, left unchanged, may lead to a possibility displayed by the card on the right.
5. End your meditation.

Exercise 4.15 – The Tarot Labyrinth

This is actually a complicated but powerful exercise that I have used with my students and it is full of symbolism. It uses all the major arcana cards in a Tarot deck spread out on a floor space. The exercise involves walking from one card to the next in numerological order (from 0 to 21 plus one more) in a pattern resembling a labyrinth. Just as the mandala is a visual device that leads you to a center, the labyrinth is a physical pathway leading to its center. The labyrinth is created by walking in a circle, then a diamond shape, followed by a triangle and then a final circle. The shapes and the number of cards within them are significant. To me, the 12 cards on the outside circle represents the zodiac and the fact that 12 represents a complete circle

(12 equal spheres will perfectly encircle a single sphere). The four cards of the diamond represent the four elements. The three cards of the triangle represent the three deities or cosmic realms (sun, moon, stars) while the inner circle represents above and below and the inner space represents center. Some Tarot decks have an additional card. I use that card as the 22nd card and I call it The Void. That card is placed inside the inner circle and is the final destination for the labyrinth. The other cards of the Major Arcana are distributed in specific places along the labyrinth's pathway according to the diagram below. The exercise is actually a series of contemplations. Starting from the beginning at the outside of the outer circle each card is approached along the path. At the station of that card, the labyrinth walker will stop and contemplate upon that particular card and then continue to the next card until the center is reached. In so doing, a deep connection to the symbolism of the cards can be made but also connections can be made between the cards. The Major Arcana can be seen as a description of a spiritual journey and only by contemplating on them in order can the deep mysteries of the spiritual journey as illustrated by the Tarot be discovered.

Just Being

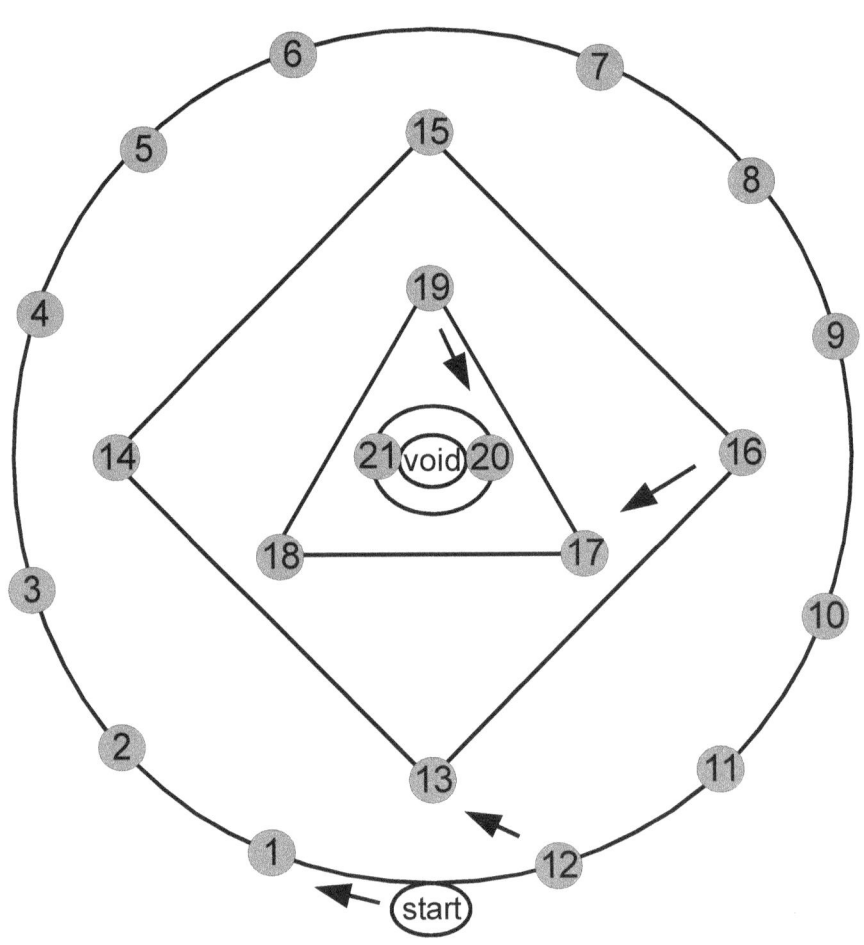

Illustration 30: A Tarot Labyrinth

Chapter Four

Exercise no.	71 (4.15)
Goal	To use all the cards of the major arcana of the Tarot in the shape of a labyrinth as a focus for contemplation.
Minimum length of time	20 minutes
Location	a large open space
Needs	a deck of Tarot cards
Steps	

1. Find a large space to create the labyrinth pattern.
2. Set your Tarot cards in the order and placement shown in the diagram above.
3. Do your outer and inner meditation procedures.
4. Starting at the lower end of the outer circle, move slowly toward the 1st Tarot card. Let your walk to the cards become part of the meditation.
5. Contemplate on the teachings of the first card. Ask how it relates to the spiritual journey and to your journey in particular.
6. When done, continue slowly to the next card position.
7. Continue until you reach the center of the circle where you can contemplate on the what you have learned from the entire journey.
8. Leave the labyrinth slowly by going out in the opposite direction.
9. End your meditation.

Exercise 4.16 – Single Rune Contemplation

Just as you did with the symbols of the Tarot cards you can use rune stones as a focus for contemplation. The Runes, however, can seem even more abstract than the artistic renderings of the Tarot. You can make your own runes or rune cards to use for this exercise. Read up on the meanings of each and then choose one for your meditation.

Exercise no.	72 (4.16)
Goal	To use a single rune stone as a focus for contemplation.
Minimum length of time	20 minutes
Location	anywhere
Needs	a rune stone
Steps	

1. Do your outer and inner meditation procedures.
2. Choose a rune stone or card.
3. Contemplate on the meaning of the symbol.
4. End your meditation.

Exercise 4.17 – The Rune Spiral

In this exercise, you will put all the rune stones in a spiral pattern on the floor and, like the labyrinth, walk from one rune to the next contemplating on both the individual runes and on the runes as a whole. Stop at each rune and meditate upon its meaning and your interpretation of it. Some rune sets have a blank or 25th rune. This rune can be placed in the center of the spiral or the center can simply be left free. The actual placement of the runes is not fixed. You do not have to put the first rune in the first position. Instead, you can mix them up and place them randomly face down in the spiral positions. This way, the meditation will be different each time. With this method you can allow your contemplation of the first encountered rune to lead to a question, the answer to which will be revealed by contemplating on the next rune to be overturned.

Chapter Four

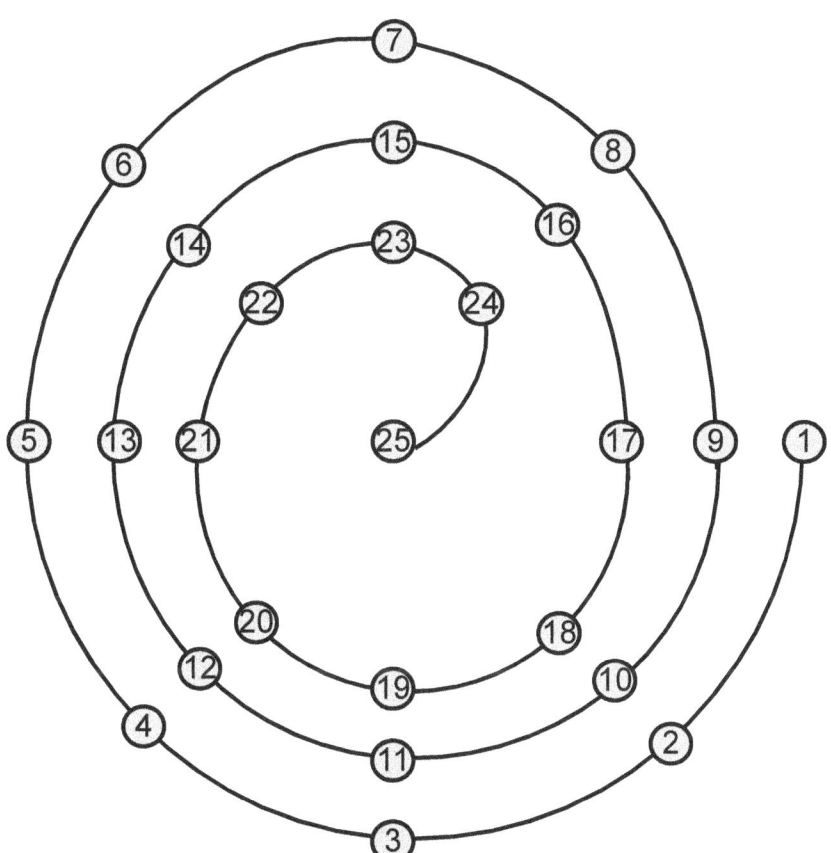

Illustration 31: A Rune Spiral

Exercise no.	73 (4.17)
Goal	To use all the runes in the shape of a spiral as a focus for contemplation.
Minimum length of time	20 minutes
Location	a large open space
Needs	a set of rune stones
Steps	

1. Randomly mix up your runes and place them face down on a floor space in the pattern above.
2. Do your outer and inner meditation procedures.
3. Begin at the first position on the spiral and turn over the first rune.
4. Contemplate upon its meaning and let it generate a question for you.
5. Move to the second spiral position and overturn the second rune placed there.
6. Meditate upon the meaning of that rune as an answer to your previous question. Let it generate another question.
7. Continue in this manner until you reach the center. Contemplate upon the meanings of all the runes you have encountered.
8. Go back through the spiral in the opposite direction picking up the runes as you go.
9. At the end of the spiral (the beginning), end your meditation.

Chapter Four

Exercise 4.18 – Single Number Contemplation

The numbers from 1 to 10 also contain specific meanings that can be used for contemplation. Take some time to study these meanings and then do a meditation to contemplate upon each one. You can use the symbol below as a mandala or guide since it contains all 10 numbers in different patterns.

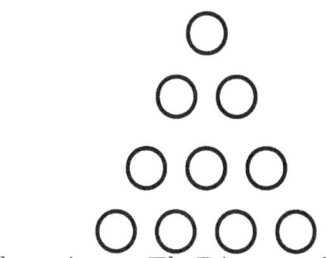

Illustration 32: The Diagram of Numbers

Exercise no.	74 (4.18)
Goal	To use the numbers from one to ten as a focus for contemplation.
Minimum length of time	20 minutes
Location	anywhere
Needs	none
Steps	

1. Review the meanings of the numbers from 1 – 10.
2. Do your outer and inner meditation procedures.
3. Contemplate on the meaning of each number beginning from 1.
4. Use the symbol above to find further meaning and connections between the numbers.
5. End your meditation.

The Symbolism of Numbers

1 The beginning, purity, potential, promise, leadership
2 The separation, transformation, change, partnerships, relationships
3 The creation, birth, synthesis, action, communication
4 The foundation, the physical, turning in, travel, meeting, home, work
5 The awakening, the emotional, loss, challenge, courage, humanity
6 The enlightenment, the mental, learning, harmony, health, contentment
7 The mystery, resolution, the spiritual, chance, connection
8 The reunion, cycles, achievements, infinity, the universe
9 The completion, attainment, contemplation, rewards, renewal, rebirth

Illustration 33: The Symbolism of Numbers

Chapter Four

Exercise 4.19 – Reduced Number Contemplation

Larger numbers can also be a source of contemplation if you reduce the number down to a number from 1 – 10. This is done by adding all the digits of a number until you get its reduction. For example, to reduce the number 6107 (the date that I am writing this), I would add the numbers 6, 1, and 7 together to get 14 (6+1+7=14). Since this is greater than 10, I would do the process again by adding together the numbers 1 and 4 to get 5 (1+4 = 5). The number 6107, then, could be reduced down to the number 5.

Exercise no.	75 (4.19)
Goal	To reduce a large number to a small number and contemplate on the significance of that number.
Minimum length of time	20 minutes
Location	anywhere
Needs	pencil and paper
Steps	

1. Choose a large number that has special significance to you such as a date, an address, or a phone number.
2. Reduce that to a number between 1 and 10.
3. Do your outer and inner meditation procedures.
4. Contemplate on the meaning of the large number in relation to the meaning of the reduced number.
5. End your meditation.

Exercise 4.20 – Gematria

Gematria is the process of assigning numbers to letters and words so that you can derive further meanings to that word. To find the number relationship of letters use the chart below, then assign a number to each letter of a chosen word. For example, the word "day" would equal 4+1+7 or 12 and the contemplation number would be 3 (1+2).

1	2	3	4	5	6	7	8	9	position
a	b	c	d	e	f	g	h	i	ones
j	k	l	m	n	o	p	q	r	tens
s	t	u	v	w	x	y	z		hundreds

Illustration 34: Number - Letter correspondences

Exercise no.	76 (4.20)
Goal	To reduce a word to a single number and contemplate on the significance of that word.
Minimum length of time	20 minutes
Location	anywhere
Needs	pencil and paper
Steps	

1. Choose a significant word to study and find its number based on the chart above.
2. Reduce the number down to a number between 1 and 10.
3. Do your outer and inner meditation procedures.
4. Contemplate upon the meaning of the word in relation to the meaning of its number.
5. End your meditation.

Chapter Four

Part Three – Emotional Meditations

The exercises in this section are meant to engage the heart. Meditations of the heart focus on love – of the self, of others, or of the divine. Adoration of a deity brings the focus of the self-absorbed ego onto a greater entity. If not approached honestly, however, deity worship can become simply a substitution for worship of the self in an idealized form. Paying honor to Spirit or to a specific deity does not mean that you can transfer your responsibilities of decency or absolve yourself of the need to be a positive member of society. By meditating upon a deity you are agreeing to worship something beyond yourself but because deity is both within and beyond you, you are also agreeing to worship the highest part of your own self.

To me, Spirit is the mysterious presence that is the source and essence of all things. It manifests itself in three powerful forces which I recognize as masculine, feminine, and neutral. The masculine is the force of Light – the need to be a separate being and the feminine is the force of Love – the need to be together. The neutral is the force of Life – the need to balance separation and unity in the struggle to become who we are. These forces can be experienced as movements of energy within the self and between others. Feeling and moving these energies involves having an open heart and a sense of Will. Moving or strengthening those energies for the benefit of yourself or others is an act of love called healing.

In these exercises, it is important to let your heart lead the way rather than your mind or body. Be open and spontaneous each time to what your heart may want you to do or feel. Honor those feelings and respond to them so long as those impulses are positive and affirming. If you feel negative or harmful impulses then you will need to immediately stop your meditation and find a way to determine why those negative feelings have arisen.

Exercise 4.21 – Masculine Energy Meditation

Consider the way in which the force of Light is expressed in yourself and all others. Open your heart and allow yourself to honor and worship this force in the universe.

Exercise no.	77 (4.21)
Goal	To contemplate on the force of Light.
Minimum length of time	20 minutes
Location	anywhere
Needs	none
Steps	

1. Do your outer and inner meditation procedures.
2. Open your heart and ask to see the force of Light within yourself.
3. Open your heart and ask to see the force of Light in all things.
4. Observe your feelings as you do this.
5. Pay honor and respect to masculine energy as your heart moves you to do.
6. Continue until you are exhausted then end your meditation.

Chapter Four

Exercise 4.22 – Feminine Energy Meditation

Consider the way in which the force of Love works to bring all beings back together. Our lives begin in Love and end in Love and in between we need Love to hold us together. Open your heart and allow yourself to worship and honor this force.

Exercise no.	78 (4.22)
Goal	To contemplate on the force of Love.
Minimum length of time	20 minutes
Location	anywhere
Needs	20 minutes
Steps	

1. Do your outer and inner meditation procedures.
2. Open your heart and ask to see the force of Love within yourself.
3. Open your heart and ask to see the force of Love in all things.
4. Observe your feelings as you do this.
5. Pay honor and respect to the feminine as your heart moves you to do.
6. Continue until you are exhausted then end your meditation.

Exercise 4.23 – Neutral Energy Meditation

Consider the way in which the force of Life works to keep us constantly balanced. Open your heart and allow yourself to worship and honor this force.

Exercise no.	79 (4.23)
Goal	To contemplate on neutral energy.
Minimum length of time	20 minutes
Location	anywhere
Needs	none
Steps	

1. Do your outer and inner meditation procedures.
2. Open your heart and ask to see the force of Light within yourself.
3. Open your heart and ask to see the force of Light in all things.
4. Observe your feelings as you do this.
5. Pay honor and respect to the neutral as your heart moves you to do.
6. Continue until you are exhausted then end your meditation.

Chapter Four

Exercise 4.24 – Earth Energies

Earth is our mother; she gives birth to us and nurtures us. Open your heart to these things by bringing in Earth energies and, thereby, feeling connected to Earth. Bring in Earth energies by pulling up energy from below you through the inward breath.

Exercise no.	80 (4.24)
Goal	To contemplate on Earth energies.
Minimum length of time	20 minutes
Location	outside on natural ground
Needs	none
Steps	

1. Do your outer and inner meditation procedures.
2. Breath slowly and fully.
3. As you breath in, feel yourself drawing up energy from the Earth from the middle of your body (the spine).
4. As you breath out, maintain that energy within you.
5. Each time you breathe in bring up more energy until you feel filled.
6. Experience how it feels to be filled with this energy.
7. When you are ready allow the energy to drain back to the Earth through the breath.
8. End your meditation.

Exercise 4.25 – Sky Energies

This exercise is the opposite of the previous exercise. You will bring down energies from the sky or the space above instead of Earth energies below you. Sky energies give us a chance to grow and shine in the light of the sun, moon, and stars. Bring in Sky energies by pulling down energy from above or around you through the inward breath.

Exercise no.	81 (4.25)
Goal	To contemplate on Sky energies.
Minimum length of time	20 minutes
Location	outside under an open sky
Needs	none
Steps	

1. Do your outer and inner meditation procedures.
2. Breath slowly and fully.
3. As you breath in feel yourself drawing down energy from the Sky or from all around you through your head and down through the middle of your body (the spine).
4. As you breath out maintain that energy within you.
5. Each time you breathe in bring down more energy until you feel filled.
6. Experience how it feels to be filled with this energy.
7. When you are ready allow the energy to rise back to the sky through the breath.
8. End your meditation.

Exercise 4.26 – Combined Earth and Sky Energies

This exercise combines the activities of the past two exercises and should only be done when both have been successfully completed. In this exercise, you will bring both Earth and Sky energies into your heart center and then extend them throughout yourself.

Exercise no.	82 (4.26)
Goal	To combine the Earth and Sky meditations.
Minimum length of time	30 minutes
Location	anywhere
Needs	none
Steps	

1. Do your outer and inner meditation procedures.
2. Breath slowly and fully.
3. As you breath in feel yourself drawing up energy from Earth and down from Sky through the middle of your body (the spine).
4. At the end of your inhalation hold your breath briefly.
5. As you hold your breath let the energies of Earth and Sky meld together in the region of your heart.
6. As you breath out let the combined energy be spread throughout your body.
7. When you are ready allow the energy to drain back to the Earth and return up to the Sky through the breath.
8. End your meditation.

Exercise 4.27 – Healing for the Self

Using the previous exercise, the energies you experienced can be used for energy healing. Healing, after all, is an act of love and Sky and Earth energies can be combined in the heart so that they can be connected to your own sense of will and caring. Though I will speak of healing here I am talking about an exercise in meditation. None of this is meant to be a practice for alternative health. Much more study and practice would be needed for that. The healing done here should be only for non-serious conditions which do not normally require the care of a healing professional such as mild headaches or minor aches and pains. Never take on any healing activities without the advise or consent of a medical or healing professional. Master the previous three exercises before doing this one.

Exercise no.	83 (4.27)
Goal	To practice healing for the self as a meditation.
Minimum length of time	30 minutes
Location	anywhere
Needs	none
Steps	

1. Do your outer and inner meditation procedures.
2. Draw in Earth and Sky energies into your heart center as you breath in and hold your breath.
3. Allow the combined energies to be moved toward the area of concern within your body with your exhalation.
4. Continue the process until you feel the area filled with energy. You may experience heat, cold, vibrations, temporary numbness or other sensations of energy.
5. Return the remaining Earth and Sky energy.
6. End your meditation.

Exercise 4.28 – Healing Others

Again, I must emphasize that this is a meditation practice and not a medical treatment for others. This should be done only with a willing partner who does not have a serious condition. Practice the Earth and Sky meditation and the self healing meditation before doing this exercise. Begin this exercise by gently placing your hands upon the part of your partner's body that is experiencing discomfort.

Exercise no.	84 (4.28)
Goal	To experience healing for others as a meditation practice.
Minimum length of time	30 minutes
Location	anywhere
Needs	someone with a mild condition
Steps	

1. Do your outer and inner meditation procedures.
2. Draw in Earth and Sky energies into your heart center as you breath in and hold your breath.
3. Allow the combined energies to be moved from your heart area down through your arms to the area of concern upon your partner's body with your exhalation.
4. Continue the process until you feel the area filled with energy. Your partner may experience heat, cold, vibrations, temporary numbness or other sensations of energy.
5. Return the remaining Earth and Sky energy.
6. End your meditation.

Just Being

Part Four – Spiritual Meditations

The meditations in this section focus on the soul. The soul is the part of the self that is closest to Spirit; it is the part which can connect to Spirit. The exercises in this section will focus on connecting with Spirit through specific Pagan symbols. One of these symbols is the four Classical elements: Earth, Air, Fire, and Water, and their correspondences. To those four we will also add the directions of Above, Below, and Center. We will also use the three celestial bodies which are also important to Pagan practice: the sun, the moon, and the stars.

Exercise 4.29 – The Cycle of the Full Moon

The full moon represents feminine energies which are receiving, nurturing, and unitive. It also represents cycles and their constant renewal to all things. On a night with a full moon, go outside and face the moon for this exercise.

Exercise no.	85 (4.29)
Goal	To connect with the cycle of the full moon.
Minimum length of time	30 minutes
Location	outdoors under a visible full moon
Needs	none
Steps	

1. Begin your outer and inner meditation procedures.
2. Look at the full moon for some time and think about the influence of feminine energies and the cycles of life.
3. Close your eyes and draw in the energy of the moon into you through your breath. Feel it strengthen the feminine part of your own energies.
4. When you are done ground any excess energies and end your meditation.

Chapter Four

Exercise 4.30 – The Cycle of the Sun

The sun represents male energies which are giving, strengthening, and empowering. The sun also represents the seasons. This exercise is most powerful when done at a solstice or equinox.

Exercise no.	86 (4.30)
Goal	To connect with the cycles of the sun.
Minimum length of time	30 minutes
Location	outdoors with the sun at a solstice or equinox
Needs	none
Steps	

1. Begin your outer and inner meditation procedures.
2. Do not look directly at the sun. Instead, observe the light of the sun as it appears around you. Think about the influence of masculine energies in you and your life.
3. Close your eyes and draw in the energy of the sun into you through your breath. Feel is strengthen the masculine part of your own energies.
4. When you are done ground any excess energies and end your meditation.

Exercise 4.31 – The Cycle of the Dark Moon

The dark moon is the time when the stars are most visible. The stars represent the neutral (neither male or female) energies which is the balance between masculine and feminine. The basis of life itself is the neutral energy which begins at rest but moves toward the masculine or feminine. Do this exercise on a night with a dark moon and a clear sky.

Exercise no.	87 (4.31)
Goal	To connect with the cycle of a dark moon.
Minimum length of time	30 minutes
Location	outdoors under a clear starry sky
Needs	none
Steps	

1. Begin your outer and inner meditation procedures.
2. Observe the stars in the night sky.
3. Think about the wonderful diversity of life and the force of balance and rest in your life and the lives of others.
4. Close your eyes and draw in the energy of the stars within.
5. When you are done ground any excess energy and end your meditation.

Chapter Four

Exercise 4.32 – The Directions: North

The following exercises will each focus on a direction and its correspondences. There are seven directions in all: North, East, South, and West (corresponding with Earth, Air, Fire, and Water) along with Above, Below, and Center. It is best to do these exercises outside in natural locations. If you can, sit on the ground or on a large rock for the Earth exercise.

Exercise no.	88 (4.32)
Goal	To connect with the direction of North and the element of Earth.
Minimum length of time	30 minutes
Location	outdoors in a natural place facing North
Needs	none
Steps	

1. Do your inner and outer meditations.
2. Face North (preferably at midnight).
3. Feel a connection between your energy and the natural Earth elements around you.
4. Experience the relationship between the Earth and your body.
5. Allow nature to teach you about Earth.
6. End your meditation.

Exercise 4.33 – The Directions: East

East is related to the element of Air and the mind. Do this exercise in a high natural place where you can experience height and can face East.

Exercise no.	89 (4.33)
Goal	To connect with the direction of East and the element of Air.
Minimum length of time	30 minutes
Location	outdoors at dawn in a high airy place
Needs	none
Steps	

7. Do your inner and outer meditations.
8. Face East (preferably at dawn).
9. Feel a connection between your energy and the breezes around you.
10. Experience the relationship between the Air and your thoughts.
11. Allow the wind to teach you about Air.
12. End your meditation.

Chapter Four

Exercise 4.34 – The Directions: South

South is related to the element of Fire and the heart. Do this exercise where you can face South and observe an open fire.

Exercise no.	90 (4.34)
Goal	To connect with the direction of South and the element of Fire.
Minimum length of time	30 minutes
Location	in a place with an open fire
Needs	a safe contained fire
Steps	

1. Do your inner and outer meditations.
2. Face South (preferably at noon).
3. Feel a connection between your energy and the fire before you.
4. Experience a relationship between Fire and your emotions.
5. Allow the Fire to teach you about your heart.
6. End your meditation.

Exercise 4.35 – The Directions: West

West is related to the element of Water and the soul. Do this exercise where you can face a body of open water.

Exercise no.	91 (4.35)
Goal	To connect with the direction of West and the element of Water.
Minimum length of time	30 minutes
Location	outdoors at dusk facing West near a body of water
Needs	none
Steps	

1. Do your inner and outer meditation procedures.
2. Face West (preferably at dusk).
3. Feel a connection between your energy and the water before you.
4. Experience a relationship between Water and your soul.
5. Allow the Water to teach your about your connection to Spirit.
6. End your meditation.

Chapter Four

Exercise 4.36 – The Directions: Below

Similar to the Earth meditation, you should do this one where you can be sitting or lying directly on the Earth. The difference with this one is that you should do it in the daylight and should focus on connecting not with singular Earth objects but with the Earth as a whole living being.

Exercise no.	92 (4.36)
Goal	To connect with the direction of below and with Mother Earth.
Minimum length of time	30 minutes
Location	a natural location during the day
Needs	none
Steps	

1. Do your outer and inner meditation procedures.
2. Lie face down upon the ground and embrace the Earth during the day.
3. Feel a connection between yourself and the Earth as a living being.
4. Allow Mother Earth to teach you about your life and your relationship to Earth.
5. End your meditation.

Exercise 4.37 – The Directions: Above

This exercise should be done in the evening while laying down on your back. Focus on connecting with all planets and stars as living entities.

Exercise no.	93 (4.37)
Goal	To connect with the direction of Above and with Father Sky.
Minimum length of time	30 minutes
Location	outdoors at night under an open sky
Needs	none
Steps	

1. Do your outer and inner meditation procedures
2. Lie face up on the ground and embrace the Sky during the night.
3. Feel a connection between yourself and the stars, planets, and all other living objects in the sky.
4. Allow Father Sky to teach you about your life and your relationship to all things beyond Earth.

Chapter Four

Exercise 4.38 – The Directions: Center

This exercise can be done anywhere. The point is that wherever you are, you are at the center of the world.

Exercise no.	94 (4.38)
Goal	To connect with the direction of Center.
Minimum length of time	30 minutes
Location	the center of the world
Needs	none
Steps	

1. Do your outer and inner meditation procedures.
2. Draw a real or imagined circle around yourself.
3. Concentrate on being at the center of the world – where the fulcrum and balance of all things meet.
4. Allow Center to teach you about balance and centering.
5. End your meditation.

Part Five – Open Meditation

All of the previous exercises have a specific focus for you to use in your practice. This exercise does not use a focus and, in fact, that is its focus. Having a focus can be a valuable aid in doing a meditation because it occupies your thoughts and allows your mind to center on something in particular. A meditation without a focus, then, can be very challenging but it can also be a very powerful form of meditation. The goal of most of the preceding exercises has been to lead you to this particular exercise. You were asked to learn to focus on something so that you can learn to focus on nothing. The goal of this exercise is not to have a totally blank mind. Instead, you are asked to have a completely open and free mind. The difference between the two is that a blank mind has no thoughts at all while an open mind may contain thoughts but those thoughts come and go freely without being a distraction. There is no thinking or processing that goes on. There is no emotional or physical reaction; there is only a connection between you and Spirit. In this meditation you want to be completely relaxed, very open, centered and connected. There is no other objective here. If you try to stop yourself from thinking or from not thinking, if you judge every thought, if you monitor every feeling and thought to see if you are doing it "right" you will be getting in the way of your own meditation.

By going through the whole text and practicing all the exercises to this point you will have come full circle. We began with exercises in which you were asked to just sit and now you have come to the last exercise which, in effect, asks you to just sit. In this case, however, you will bring to your sitting a variety of meditative experiences and the wisdom you have developed along the way. Development takes place in a spiral. You have not just come full circle, you have circled around the spiral to a higher level. Hopefully, this will be but one of many trips along your spiral of development.

Chapter Four

Exercise 4.39 – Open Meditation

Unlike all all the other exercises in this book, the focus of this meditation is to have no focus while keeping your mind completely open.

Exercise no.	95 (4.39)
Goal	To meditate with no focus.
Minimum length of time	one hour
Location	anywhere
Needs	none
Steps	

1. Do your outer and inner meditation procedures.
2. Sit and practice breathing very fully and slowly.
3. Allow your mind to be completely free and open.
4. If thoughts, sensations, or feelings come to you simply allow them to come and go.
5. Feel a sense of complete peace and serenity around you.
6. Continue for as long as you can and then end your meditation.

Just Being

Chapter Five
Beyond Meditation

Introduction

There are things involved with meditation that go beyond the practice of sitting and focusing. Like any practice, there are a variety of tools that can be employed. There are special pieces of clothing, equipment to sit on, altars and all their tools, music, and many other items that can be purchased or made for use during your meditation practice. One of the most important and most useful of these tools is the meditation journal – a place to record your thoughts and experiences. Nearly all meditation traditions emphasize the use of a practice journal. Its real use and meaning only becomes clear, however, after many months and years of using one.

Looking beyond the meditation practice means more than just seeking cool stuff and writing meditation notes. It is possible to take meditation to another level. For the novice meditator, meditation is something that is done regularly for a limited time but for the advanced meditator, life itself as a meditation. This type of attitude allows a person to see every moment, action, and interaction as a chance to practice and deepen his or her practice. All activities become mindful active meditations. All quiet or otherwise dull moments (like standing in line somewhere) become a chance to practice focusing the mind. Dealings with other people become a chance to practice an open heart and compassion. Moments of sitting meditation become a chance to remind one's self of how to live and act during the non-sitting times. For Pagans, living meditation means taking every chance to recognize Spirit in all things, to love Earth and all beings, to practice an avoidance of harm, and to celebrate the natural cycles of life.

Part One – Meditation Tools

Besides an altar there are many other kinds of tools that can be used in a meditation practice. Some objects have already been mentioned earlier in this text when they were used for specific meditations. Those objects included the mandala, the prayer bead, the prayer shawl, the candle, and the bell, just to name a few. There are other tools which can be useful in a meditation practice. These can include things like a meditation cushion, a timer, music, or special clothing. There are a variety of cushions available for meditation. You can buy any cushion at a retail store or you can purchase cushions made especially for sitting meditations. Zen Buddhists often use a cushion called a *zafu* which is designed for sitting in meditation for long periods of time. There are even special benches and chairs made for meditation. A timer can be useful if you are trying to extend your meditation times but it can also be disruptive. Timers should be used when first learning to meditate but, eventually, the meditation should be done without regard to time. Keeping a timer nearby without activating the sound can be useful for marking the length of a meditation session when you have finished.

Some people prefer to meditate in silence while others prefer music. The right choice of music can influence your state of mind but it can also have the disadvantage of influencing your emotions in a different direction than the one you chose for your focus. The choice of music is very important. It needs to match closely the experience you are trying to obtain in your practice. Another disadvantage of using music is that it exists in a finite time (unless you put it on a continuous loop) which may or may not correspond to the length of time for your meditation. Music can be used as a kind of gentle timer, however. Some people also prefer to meditate using special clothing such as a cape, a prayer shawl, a robe, or a special outfit. Using special clothing helps put your body and mind into a different mindset. When you put on your meditation shawl, for example, you are telling your mind and body that it is time to prepare for meditation and to separate yourself from your everyday thoughts and concerns. The clothing you choose should be used only when you meditate and should be loose and comfortable.

One of the most important meditation tools is the meditation journal. The journal can be a simple notebook or a fancy leather bound tome. It can be done on a computer or hand written. You can make it any way you like. The important thing is to keep one and to make entries in it every time you practice. A meditation journal helps you put into words the experiences you had during the meditation. It is important to keep your journal nearby when you practice so that you can write in it as soon as you have finished. In each of the exercises in this book you should consider writing in your journal as soon as you end your meditation. Keeping a journal gives you a chance to look back over your previous sessions and observe your progress. It also gives you a chance to make a further analysis of what you have done and can allow you to make connections between different experiences and discoveries you might not have made otherwise. Making progress in meditation can seem painfully slow. Sometimes it seems not to happen at all. Though there may be times when you get instant flashes of wisdom and enlightenment, most of the time development is very slow. Sometimes you will not notice that development until you review past notes and see where you may have been some time ago.

Sometimes people have every intention of keeping a journal but do not know what to write. They pick up the pen and then just stare at the empty page. Their minds become as blank as the page itself. If you are one of those people then I suggest that you have a format to follow. Create a list of information and questions you can use to inspire you to write. A typical format to follow would be to write in your journal using at least three categories: the main information, the description, and the analysis of the session. The main information would include the date and location of your session, how much time you spent meditating (include a start time and an end time), and a listing of the primary goal of the session. The description should be a set of brief narratives. The first should describe what exactly you did in your session. Describe the methods you used to achieve your goal. Be as specific as you can in case you want to recreate the same method again later. The second narrative should be about what you experienced during your session. Write your thoughts and feelings about what happened while you were meditating even if you felt like nothing at all happened. Try to be descriptive without being judgmental. The third narrative should include a description of what you learned from your experience. You may have had some deep and exciting insights or you may have experienced nothing. In either case, you learned something even if that something is that you should not do that particular type of meditation again.

The third part of your journal entry should be a brief analysis of the session. Ask yourself how the meditation worked for you. Try to keep your judgments as to whether or not the particular method was helpful to you or not rather than judging whether or not you were good at it. It is never helpful to determine that you failed or were inadequate in your session. As long as you try, you are making progress; as long as you are sincere, you are where you should be in your development. Have faith and determination to continue your practice regardless of whether or not you think you are getting it right. Next, write about how the session related to things you learned and experienced in previous sessions or to things you may have experienced since you last sat down to meditate. Finally, write a short section on what you could do next time to make your meditation session even more effective or what you think your next goal should be in relation to what you just learned or experienced. There is an example of a meditation journal format in the appendices.

Part Two – Life As A Meditation

Meditation can profoundly affect your whole life especially if you decide to use it for just that purpose. Meditation can be a type of rehearsal to practice thinking and feeling like the person you want to become. If you find that you are not the person you really want to be – for whatever reason – you can meditate on finding and becoming that person. The first step is to determine who or what you want to be. To do this, it helps to have a model. Your model can be a real person like someone you have met who you greatly respect and admire. Observe that person and notice how he or she acts in different situations. Take note of those positive characteristics so that you can adapt them for yourself. You could also use a deity, mythical, or heroic figure for your model. Whether or not the person is real does not matter. If you can imagine this deity or person in various situations then you can emulate those characteristics. In some ways it is better to have a more-than-human model so that you will always have a higher goal to reach. You could also create a personality as a model. This person would be the ultimate you – the you that you want to become. Through your meditations you would practice being this person in all the different types of activities you normally do. In this way you become deity. You have heard the phrase "What would Jesus do?" This is the same idea except that you could replace the name with any name you would like. You could ask "what would Apollo do" or "what would Kwan-Yin do." You might also ask what would my teacher do or what would my higher self do? These are good questions to ask but what you really want to ask is "what would I do as that person?" This recognizes that you respect and wish to emulate another figure but that you are still yourself and have to adapt to that reality. You cannot actually do what Apollo or Kwan-Yin or Master Mike or Billy the Grocer would do. You can only do what the greater and higher part of yourself can do in emulation of that person. But, that higher part of yourself is capable of more than you may realize.

By emulating others and finding models for your higher self, you begin to act as the person you want to be. There will be many moments when you will slip back into the old person but constant vigilance and practice will help keep you on your new path. When you do this you are more than just being deity, you are living deity. Living in this way is purely natural and good because you are deity. You are one part – one spark – of the totality of Spirit and you are no less sacred than any other. If you are so divine, then why not act divine? Imagine what it would be like to live and act divine and then imagine yourself acting in that way. If you can see yourself as a deity then you can also see others as divine as well. What would it be like to treat all others as if they were also divine? Of course, not all people always act in divine ways but could we be more tolerant and forgiving if we separated the actions from the person? Even mythological heroes have been known to do stupid things. Imagine what it would be like to be a god or goddess in a world of gods and goddesses who do not always

Imagine what it would be like to live and act divine and then imagine yourself acting in that way.

act so divine.

Another way to use meditation in everyday life is to be able to recall the peaceful gentle state of mind that you developed in your practice while in stressful times. For example, how many times have you been in a less-than-friendly conversation with someone and you spoke out quickly in anger only to later regret what you said? Sometimes it helps to put a little space between what comes your way and what you return. Try to wait a bit before responding and enter into your peaceful space where you can briefly collect your thoughts and calm yourself. If you need to remind yourself of this space by using a mantra or mudra then do so. Anytime you find yourself in a stressful situation it can be helpful to enter into that peaceful place you have developed. You may not be able to change the immediate situation but learning to be peaceful will help you to better deal with difficult situations.

For some, meditation is a hobby. It may be a serious hobby and it may important but it is still a part-time activity. For a few others, meditation is a way of life: all parts of the self are involved in some form of meditative engagement and all actions become a chance to practice mindfulness. The more mundane and seemingly boring the activity, the more it becomes a chance to engage the body and center the mind. All thoughts become either a contemplation or a mantra. Every opportunity is sought to cease thoughts and experience inner silence and peace. Every interaction with another person or being becomes a chance to practice compassion. Every place, every object, every thing everywhere becomes a chance to recognize the beauty of Spirit and to experience a connection between yourself and all things. Every moment becomes a chance to practice complete awareness of the joy and wonder of living.

Exercises

These exercises are long term meditations. They are meant to be done through the course of at least one day or more. Each one begins with a morning meditation and then a follow-through for the day. For each, you should carry with you something to constantly remind yourself of your goal for the day. Such an item can be a stone or charm or even just a piece of paper with your goal written upon it.

Chapter Five

Keep the object near to you through the day. To bless the object, you can simply say a chant or mantra over it or you might actually write upon it.

Exercise 5.1 - Becoming Deity

In order to do this exercise you must first have set clearly in your mind an image of a deity or model figure. Ask yourself how this person or entity would act in many different situations.

Exercise no.	96 (5.1)
Goal	To emulate deity as a meditation.
Minimum length of time	a full day
Location	anywhere
Needs	
Steps	

1. Do your outer and inner meditation procedures.
2. Clearly see in your mind the image of the deity or person you have chosen.
3. Have that person go through a typical day of yours in your mind.
4. See yourself as that person and go through the same imaginary day acting in the way you wish to be.
5. Use a sacred object to remind yourself of your goal to act in the manner of your chosen model.
6. Bless that object and fuse it with your intent.
7. End your meditation and use the remainder of the day to practice being the person you have chosen to be.

Exercise 5.2 – Mindful Actions

With this exercise, all actions become a chance to practice mindfulness. In mindfulness you are focused solely upon the activity you are doing and nothing else.

Exercise no.	97 (5.2)
Goal	To do all actions in a mindful state.
Minimum length of time	a full day
Location	anywhere
Needs	none
Steps	

1. Do your outer and inner meditation procedures.
2. See in your mind an image of yourself doing your common activities.
3. See yourself doing those activities mindfully.
4. Use a sacred object to remind yourself of your goal to do all activities mindfully.
5. Bless that object and fuse it with your intent.
6. End your meditation and use the remainder of the day to practice doing all activities with mindfulness.

Exercise 5.3 – The Quiet Mind

This will be a challenging exercise if you are like many people who have difficulty stilling their minds. To do this exercise throughout the day it will be important for you to distinguish which thoughts are necessary in your life and which may be frivolous. Allow the important thoughts and decisions to become a means for contemplation. In other words, focus your concentration on that thought or problem until you have found an answer or the thought becomes no longer necessary. When unnecessary thoughts appear, allow them to come and go without processing them. Focus on having a quiet and still mind throughout the day.

Exercise no.	98 (5.3)
Goal	To maintain a quiet mind as a meditation.
Minimum length of time	one full day
Location	anywhere
Needs	none
Steps	

1. Do your outer and inner meditation procedures.
2. Practice quieting your mind allowing thoughts to just come and go like leaves that roll by in the wind.
3. See yourself practicing a quiet mind throughout the day.
4. Use a sacred object to remind yourself of your goal to keep a quiet mind.
5. Bless that object and fuse it with your intent.
6. End your meditation and use the remainder of the day to practice having a quiet mind.

Exercise 5.4 – Promoting Compassion

Compassion means having an open heart toward yourself and all others. Being compassionate does not mean to not also be safe. You can have an open heart without putting yourself in danger or a compromising situation. You can be compassionate and still say no. Caring about others more does not come at the price of caring for yourself less. Both should be equal. Imagine acting in ways that are compassionate to others as well as to yourself.

Exercise no.	99 (5.4)
Goal	To maintain an open heart as a meditation.
Minimum length of time	one full day
Location	anywhere
Needs	none
Steps	

1. Do your outer and inner meditation procedures.
2. Practice opening your heart to yourself and all beings.
3. Seeing yourself acting compassionate throughout the day.
4. Use a sacred object to remind yourself of your goal to be compassionate.
5. Bless that object and fuse it with your intent.
6. End your meditation and use the remainder of the day to practice compassion to yourself and all beings.

Chapter Five

Exercise 5.5 – Connecting to All Things

We spend our days feeling separated from each other and sometimes even from ourselves. We are meant to be independent beings because that is how we stay in motion and interact with our world. It is this constant interaction and our experience of living that keeps Spirit alive. Spirit lives through us and we live through it. The problem with this reality is that we can forget that we are really all part of one body. That body is not physical but spiritual. Try to spend a day seeing yourself connected to all things rather than being separate. Like leaves on a tree, we may each wave in the wind and yearn for sunlight in our own ways but, in reality, we are all connected to the same tree. See yourself connected to an invisible spiritual tether.

Exercise no.	100 (5.5)
Goal	To maintain a connection to all things as a meditation.
Minimum length of time	one full day
Location	anywhere
Needs	none
Steps	

1. Do your outer and inner meditation procedures.
2. Practice seeing yourself connected to all beings and all things.
3. See yourself finding that connection all through the day.
4. Use a sacred object to remind yourself of your goal to see that all pervasive connection.
5. Bless that object and fuse it with your intent.
6. End your meditation and use the remainder of the day to practice seeing and experiencing your connection to all people, all beings, and all things.

Just Being

Appendices

A Group Pagan Cakes and Tea Ceremony

This is a version of the Pagan Cakes and Tea exercise found in Chapter Four but has been written for use with a group. It appeals to all the senses and is a good group meditation in that each person can do as much or as little as he or she likes.

Sensual experiences:
- taste: food and drink
- smell: the food and flowers, the candle
- touch: warm cloth
- visual: table setting with small pieces of art
- aural: soft music

Needs:
- tea bags
- cookies or other finger food
- teacups and saucers
- small plates
- face cloths
- teapot
- music player and appropriate music
- bell or gong, large bowl
- a plate or bowl containing an assortment of tea bags
- chalice

Preparation:
- Set table or area with:
  - a tablecloth
  - flowers
  - some pieces of artwork or crafts

- candle
- sugar and cream
- a chalice
➢ Give each place setting:
  - a small plate
  - a saucer
  - a spoon
  - face cloth
➢ Leader should have:
  - matches
  - teapot or something to warm water
  - fragrant oil (optional)
  - large washing bowl
  - plate of tea bags
  - teacups

The Ceremony:
1. Seat your guests and start the music.
   a) instruct them on the ceremony.
   b) ask them to be silent between the ringing of the bells (except for the blessings).
2. Ring the bell.
3. Light the candle and express your intent.
4. Bow to each other and sit quietly for a moment.
5. Leader pours some warm water into a large bowl. (a fragrant oil may be added)
6. Leader passes the bowl to his or her left and says "May you and all those you touch be blessed."
7. The receiving person bows to the offering then dips his or hand into the bowl and moistens hands and face. He or she then dries hands and face with the face cloth then passes on the bowl with the same blessing. Continue until all have done the same. (The Leader will be the last to dip hands into the bowl.)
8. The leader begins passing the bowl of tea bags in the same manner with the words "I honor you with this gift. Continue until all have chosen a tea bag.
9. The leader will fill teacups with warm water and pass them one at a time. Each person should offer each teacup with a bow and

each should be received with a bow until all persons have a filled teacup.
10. The leader will then raise his or her teabag and the others will follow. The leader will say "We bless this water with the flowers of the Earth. Let it nourish our souls." The participants dip their tea bag to their liking but do not drink.
11. The leader takes the chalice in left hand and raises teacup in right hand and says "From Earth we receive, to Earth we return." He or she pours a very small amount of tea into the chalice and then passes the chalice on in the same manner as before. Each person does the same. Continue until all have made the blessing.
12. The leader holds up the cup of tea and says "May we receive this gift of the Earth with gratitude and may we return that gratitude through our good works." All drink the tea together.
13. The leader begins passing the small treats around the circle in the same manner as before and. Continue until all have received the food.
14. The leader holds up the food and says "May we be thankful for this time to be here together." Participants eat and finish their tea.
15. When all have finished, leader bows to group and group returns the bow.
16. Ring the bell and end the ceremony.

A Meditation Journal Format

The following chart can be used as a format for writing in your meditation journal after each session. This is designed for those who may have difficulty determining what should be written in a meditation journal and are looking for further guidance.

I. Main Information		
	A. Date	
	B. Location	
	C. Start time	
	D. End time	
	E. Primary Goal	
II. Description		
	A. Procedure:	
	B. Your experience:	
III. Analysis		
	A. Was the meditation successful?	
	B. What did you learn?	
	C. How does it relate to previous practices?	
	D. How does it relate to your life?	

Appendices

E. How could this meditation be improved?	

Just Being

A Meditation Practice Check-Off Sheet

For those who wish to go through all the exercises in this book I have provided a check-off list for each chapter.

1. Preface
    - ☐ 📖 Preliminary Exercise 1
    - ☐ 📖 Preliminary Exercise 2
    - ☐ 📖 Preliminary Exercise 3

2. Chapter One - Basic Meditation
    - ☐ 📖 Exercise 1 (1.1) – Just Sitting
    - ☐ 📖 Exercise 2 (1.2) – Follow Your Breathing
    - ☐ 📖 Exercise 3 (1.3) – 15 Second Meditation
    - ☐ 📖 Exercise 4 (1.4) – 30 Second Meditation
    - ☐ 📖 Exercise 5 (1.5) – 1 Minute Meditation

3. Chapter Two – The Outer Procedure
    a) Stretching
    - ☐ 📖 Exercise 6 (2.1) - Basic Stretch
    - ☐ 📖 Exercise 7 (2.2) – Basic Stretch with Breathing
    - ☐ 📖 Exercise 8 (2.3) – Sitting Stretch
    - ☐ 📖 Exercise 9A (2.4) – Pagan Tai Chi (setting the layers)
    - ☐ 📖 Exercise 9B (2.4) Pagan Tai Chi (setting the four directions)
    - ☐ 📖 Exercise 10 (2.5) – Sun Salutation

    b) Centering
    - ☐ 📖 Exercise 11 (2.6) – Centering With The Floor
    - ☐ 📖 Exercise 12 (2.7) – Adding The Breath

    c) Connecting
    - ☐ 📖 Exercise 13 (2.8) – The Tree
    - ☐ 📖 Exercise 14 (2.9) – The Translucent Ball

    d) Entering In
    - ☐ 📖 Exercise 15 (2.10) – The Inner Temple

    e) Invocation and Release
    - ☐ 📖 Exercise 16 (2.11) – Invocation and Release

    f) Intent

Appendices

- ☐ Exercise 17 (2.12) – Intent and Acknowledgment
g) Putting It All Together
- ☐ Exercise 18 (2.13) – The Outer Meditation Procedure

4. Chapter Three – The Inner Procedure
   a) Relaxation
   - ☐ Exercise 19 (3.1) – Tensing Muscles
   - ☐ Exercise 20 (3.2) – Visualization
   - ☐ Exercise 21 (3.3) – Progressive Relaxation I: Sitting
   - ☐ Exercise 22 (3.4) – Progressive Relaxation II: Breathing
   - ☐ Exercise 23 (3.5) – The Body Scan
   - ☐ Exercise 24 (3.6) – Deep Relaxation
   - ☐ Exercise 25 (3.7) – The Relaxation Mantra
   - ☐ Exercise 26 (3.8) – The Relaxation Mudra
   b) Concentration
   - ☐ Exercise 27 (3.9) – Observing The Mind
   - ☐ Exercise 28 (3.10) – Clearing The Mind
   - ☐ Exercise 29 (3.11) – Relaxing The Mind
   - ☐ Exercise 30 (3.12) – Visual Concentration
   - ☐ Exercise 31 (3.13) – Aural Concentration: Music
   - ☐ Exercise 32 (3.14) – Aural Concentration: Chanting
   - ☐ Exercise 33 (3.15) – Aural Concentration: The Bell
   - ☐ Exercise 34 (3.16) – Contemplation: Who Am I?
   - ☐ Exercise 35 (3.17) – Contemplation: Sacred Reading
   - ☐ Exercise 36 (3.18) – Contemplation: The Silent Om
   - ☐ Exercise 37 (3.19) – Mindfulness
   - ☐ Exercise 38 (3.20) – The Concentration Mantra
   - ☐ Exercise 39 (3.21) – The Concentration Mudra
   c) Acceptance
   - ☐ Exercise 40 (3.22) – Acceptance of the Self: Taking Inventory
   - ☐ Exercise 41 (3.23) – Acceptance of the Self: An Affirmation
   - ☐ Exercise 42 (3.24) – Acceptance of Others: Taking Inventory
   - ☐ Exercise 43 (3.25) – Acceptance of Others: An

Affirmation
- ☐ Exercise 44 (3.26) - Acceptance of All: Taking Inventory
- ☐ Exercise 45 (3.27) – Acceptance of All: An Affirmation
- ☐ Exercise 46 (3.28) – Pagan Loving-kindness
- ☐ Exercise 47 (3.29) – The Acceptance Mantra
- ☐ Exercise 48 (3.30) – The Acceptance Mudras

d) Absorption
- ☐ Exercise 49 (3.31) – Slowing Time
- ☐ Exercise 50 (3.32) – Self-Expansion
- ☐ Exercise 51 (3.33) – Self Dissolution
- ☐ Exercise 52 (3.34) – Entering Flow
- ☐ Exercise 53 (3.35) – The Absorption Mantra
- ☐ Exercise 54 (3.36) – The Absorption Mudra

e) Combined Procedure
- ☐ Exercise 55 (3.37) – The Combined Inner Procedure
- ☐ Exercise 56 (3.38) – The Combined Outer and Inner Procedures

5. Chapter Four – Pagan Meditations
  a) Physical Meditations
  - ☐ Exercise 57 (4.1) – Making Pagan Prayer Beads
  - ☐ Exercise 58 (4.2) – Using Pagan Prayer Beads
  - ☐ Exercise 59 (4.3) – Making A Meditation Shawl
  - ☐ Exercise 60 (4.4) – Using A Meditation Shawl
  - ☐ Exercise 61 (4.5) – Chanting
  - ☐ Exercise 62 (4.6) – Sacred Dancing
  - ☐ Exercise 63 (4.7) – Sacred Drumming
  - ☐ Exercise 64 (4.8) – Creating Your Own Mandala
  - ☐ Exercise 65 (4.9) – The Pentagram Walk
  - ☐ Exercise 66 (4.10) – The Cakes and Tea Ceremony

  b) Mental Meditations
  - ☐ Exercise 67 (4.11) – Contemplation on the Pentagram
  - ☐ Exercise 68 (4.12) – A Pagan Mandala
  - ☐ Exercise 69 (4.13) – Single Tarot Card Contemplation

Appendices

- ☐ Exercise 70 (4.14) – Multiple Tarot Card Contemplation
- ☐ Exercise 71 (4.15) – The Tarot Labyrinth
- ☐ Exercise 72 (4.16) – Single Rune Contemplation
- ☐ Exercise 73 (4.17) – The Rune Spiral
- ☐ Exercise 74 (4.18) – Single Number Contemplation
- ☐ Exercise 75 (4.19) – Reduced Number Contemplation
- ☐ Exercise 76 (4.20) – Gematria

c) Emotional Meditations

- ☐ Exercise 77 (4.21) – Masculine Energy Meditation
- ☐ Exercise 78 (4.22) – Feminine Energy Meditation
- ☐ Exercise 79 (4.23) – Neutral Energy Meditation
- ☐ Exercise 80 (4.24) – Earth Energies
- ☐ Exercise 81 (4.25) – Sky Energies
- ☐ Exercise 82 (4.26) – Combined Earth and Sky Energies
- ☐ Exercise 83 (4.27) – Healing for the Self
- ☐ Exercise 84 (4.28) – Healing Others

d) Spiritual Meditations

- ☐ Exercise 85 (4.29) – The Cycle of the The Full Moon
- ☐ Exercise 86 (4.30) – The Cycle of the Sun
- ☐ Exercise 87 (4.31) – The Cycle of the Dark Moon
- ☐ Exercise 88 (4.32) – The Directions: North
- ☐ Exercise 89 (4.33) – The Directions: East
- ☐ Exercise 90 (4.34) – The Directions: South
- ☐ Exercise 91 (4.35) – The Directions: West
- ☐ Exercise 92 (4.36) – The Directions: Below
- ☐ Exercise 93 (4.37) – The Directions: Above
- ☐ Exercise 94 (4.38) – The Directions: Center

e) Open Meditation

- ☐ Exercise 95 (4.39) – Open Meditation

6. Chapter Five – Beyond Meditation
    - ☐ Exercise 96 (5.1) – Becoming Deity
    - ☐ Exercise 97 (5.2) – Mindful Actions
    - ☐ Exercise 98 (5.3) – The Quiet Mind

Just Being

- ☐ Exercise 99 (5.4) – Promoting Compassion
- ☐ Exercise 100 (5.5) – Connecting To All Things

Appendices

Resources

Source Books

Dabrowski, Kazimierz. *Positive Disintegration*. Little, Brown and Company, 1964.

Dass, Ram. *Journey of Awakening*. Bantam Books, 1990.

Goleman, Daniel. *The Meditative Mind: The Varieties of Meditative Experience*. Jeremy P. Tarcher, Inc, 1977.

Hahn, Thich Nhat. *Peace Is Every Step*. Bantam Books, 1991.

Humphrey, Naomi. *Meditation: The Inner Way*. The Aquarian Press, 1987.

Jou, Tsung Hwa. *The Tao of Tai Chi Chuan*. Tai Chi Foundation, 1988.

Kotsias, John. *The Essential Movements of Tai Chi*. Paradigm Publications, 1989.

LeShan, Lawrence. *How To Meditate: A Guide To Self Discovery*. Little, Brown and Company, 1974.

Levey, Joel and Michelle. *The Fine Arts of Relaxation, Concentration, and Meditation*. Wisdom Publications, 1991.

Lidell, Lucy. *The Sivananda Companion to Yoga*. Simon and Schuster, 1983.

Patanjali. *The Yoga Sutras*.

Paulson, Genevieve L. *Meditation As Spiritual Practice*. Llewellyn Publications, 2006.

Underhill, Evelyn. *Mysticism: The Nature and Development of Spiritual Consciousness*. Oneworld Publications, 1993.

Related Books

Ash, Steven and Renate. *Sacred Drumming.*

Baldwin, Christina. *Life's Companion: Journal Writing as a Spiritual Practice.*

Berres, Janet. *Tarot Kit For Beginners.*

Davis, Martha and Matthew McKay, Elizabeth Robbins Eshelman. *The Relaxation & Stress Reduction Workbook.*

Drayer, Ruth. *Numerology: The Power in Numbers.*

Fontana, David. *Meditating with Mandalas: 52 New Mandalas to Help You Grow in Peace and Awareness.*

Gass, Robert and Kathleen A. Brehony. *Chanting: Discovering Spirit in Sound.*

Izard, Susan S. and Susan S. Jorgensen. *Knitting into the Mystery: A Guide to the Shawl-Knitting Ministry.*

Kabat-Zinn, Jon. *Mindfulness for Beginners.*

Moore, Thomas. *Dark Night of the Soul.*

St. John of the Cross. *Dark Night of the Soul.*

Thorsson, Edred. *Futhark: A Handbook of Rune Magic.*

Watts, June. *Circle Dancing: Celebrating the Sacred in Dance.*

Wood, Ernest. *Concentration: An Approach to Meditation.*

Zukav, Gary and Linda Francis. *Thoughts from the Heart of the Soul: Meditations on Emotional Awareness.*

Appendices

Web Pages

The Skillful Meditation Project - http://www.meditationproject.org

Institute for Applied Meditation - http://www.appliedmeditation.org

Naropa University - http://www.naropa.edu

Shawl Ministry - http://www.shawlministry.com

Universal Dances of Peace – http://www.dancesofuniversalpeace.org

The Meaning of the Pentagram -
http://www.witchvox.com/va/dt_va.html?a=usma&c=basics&id=2875

Indices

Exercises

Preliminary Exercise 1 19
Preliminary Exercise 2 20
Preliminary Exercise 3 20
Exercise 1.1 – Just Sitting 46
Exercise 1.2 – Just Breathing 47
Exercise 1.3 – 15 Second Meditation 48
Exercise 1.4 – 30 Second Meditation 48
Exercise 1.5 – 1 Minute Meditation 49
Exercise 2.1 – Basic stretch 68
Exercise 2.2 – The Basic Stretch With Breathing 70
Exercise 2.3 – Sitting Stretch 73
Exercise 2.4 – Pagan Tai Chi 76
Exercise 2.5 The Sun Salutation 80
Exercise 2.6 – Centering With The Floor 82
Exercise 2.7 – Adding the Breath 83
Exercise 2.8 – The Tree 84
Exercise 2.9 – The Translucent Ball 85
Exercise 2.10 – The Inner Temple 86
Exercise 2.11 – Invocation and Release 89
Exercise 2.12 – Intent and Acknowledgment 91
Exercise 2.13 – The Outer Meditation Procedure 92
Exercise 3.1 – Tensing Muscles 108
Exercise 3.2 – Visualization 109
Exercise 3.3 – Progressive Relaxation I: Sitting 110
Exercise 3.4 – Progressive Relaxation II: Breathing 111
Exercise 3.5 – The Body Scan 112
Exercise 3.6 – Deep Relaxation 113
Exercise 3.7 – The Relaxation Mantra 114
Exercise 3.8 – The Relaxation Mudra 115
Exercise 3.9 – Observing the Mind 116
Exercise 3.10 – Clearing the Mind 117
Exercise 3.11 – Relaxing the Mind 118
Exercise 3.12 – Visual Concentration 119
Exercise 3.13 – Aural Concentration: Music 121
Exercise 3.14 – Aural Concentration: Chanting 122

Appendices

Exercise 3.15 – Aural Concentration: The Bell..................................124
Exercise 3.16 – Contemplation: Who Am I?..124
Exercise 3.17 – Contemplation: Sacred Reading................................125
Exercise 3.18 – Contemplation: The Silent Om..................................126
Exercise 3.19 – Mindfulness..127
Exercise 3.20 – The Concentration Mantra...128
Exercise 3.21 – The Concentration Mudra..130
Exercise 3.22 – Acceptance of the Self: Taking Inventory................132
Exercise 3.23 – Acceptance of the Self: An Affirmation...................134
Exercise 3.24 – Acceptance of Others: Taking Inventory.................135
Exercise 3.25: Acceptance of Others: An Affirmation......................137
Exercise 3.26 – Accepting All: Taking Inventory..............................138
Exercise 3.27 – Acceptance of All: An Affirmation..........................140
Exercise 3.28 – Pagan Loving-Kindness...141
Exercise 3.29 – The Acceptance Mantra...145
Exercise 3.30 – The Acceptance Mudras...145
Exercise 3.31 – Slowing Time...147
Exercise 3.32 – Self Expansion...148
Exercise 3.33 – Self Dissolution...149
Exercise 3.34 – Entering Flow..151
Exercise 3.35 – The Absorption Mantra...152
Exercise 3.36 – The Absorption Mudra..152
Exercise 3.37 – The Combined Inner Procedure...............................154
Exercise 3.38 – The Combined Outer and Inner Procedures..........154
Exercise 4.1 – Making Pagan Prayer Beads.......................................158
Exercise 4.2 – Using Pagan Prayer Beads..164
Exercise 4.3 – Making a Meditation Shawl..165
Exercise 4.4 - Using a Meditation Shawl..166
Exercise 4.5 – Chanting..167
Exercise 4.6 – Sacred Dancing...168
Exercise 4.7 – Sacred Drumming..169
Exercise 4.8 – Creating Your Own Mandala.....................................170
Exercise 4.9 – The Pentagram Walk...171
Exercise 4.10 – The Cakes and Tea Ceremony..................................172
Exercise 4.11 – Contemplation on the Pentagram............................174
Exercise 4.12 – A Pagan Mandala...175
Exercise 4.13 – Single Tarot Card Contemplation............................177
Exercise 4.14 – Multiple Tarot Card Contemplation.......................178

237

Exercise 4.15 – The Tarot Labyrinth..178
Exercise 4.16 – Single Rune Contemplation..182
Exercise 4.17 – The Rune Spiral..182
Exercise 4.18 – Single Number Contemplation....................................185
Exercise 4.19 – Reduced Number Contemplation.................................187
Exercise 4.20 – Gematria..188
Exercise 4.21 – Masculine Energy Meditation.....................................190
Exercise 4.22 – Feminine Energy Meditation......................................191
Exercise 4.23 – Neutral Energy Meditation..192
Exercise 4.24 – Earth Energies..193
Exercise 4.25 – Sky Energies...194
Exercise 4.26 – Combined Earth and Sky Energies..............................195
Exercise 4.27 – Healing for the Self...196
Exercise 4.28 – Healing Others...197
Exercise 4.29 – The Cycle of the Full Moon..198
Exercise 4.30 – The Cycle of the Sun...199
Exercise 4.31 – The Cycle of the Dark Moon......................................200
Exercise 4.32 – The Directions: North...201
Exercise 4.33 – The Directions: East..202
Exercise 4.34 – The Directions: South...203
Exercise 4.35 – The Directions: West...204
Exercise 4.36 – The Directions: Below...205
Exercise 4.37 – The Directions: Above...206
Exercise 4.38 – The Directions: Center..207
Exercise 4.39 – Open Meditation..209
Exercise 5.1 - Becoming Deity..217
Exercise 5.2 – Mindful Actions...218
Exercise 5.3 – The Quiet Mind...219
Exercise 5.4 – Promoting Compassion...220
Exercise 5.5 – Connecting to All Things...221

Appendices

Illustrations

Illustration 1: The Equilateral Cross	30
Illustration 2: Levels of Physical Relaxation	31
Illustration 3: Sine Waves	32
Illustration 4: Brain Wave Patterns	32
Illustration 5: Levels of Emotional Growth	34
Illustration 6: Levels of Spiritual Growth	35
Illustration 7: Comparison of Levels	36
Illustration 8: A Hermetic Cosmogony of the Elements	37
Illustration 9: The Non-Material to The Material	38
Illustration 10: Progression of the Parts of Self	39
Illustration 11: The Spheres of Relationships	44
Illustration 12: Meditative Goals	45
Illustration 13: Meditation Positions	60
Illustration 14: The Inner and Outer Procedures	62
Illustration 15: Outer Procedure Steps	63
Illustration 16: Meditation Invocation	90
Illustration 17: Parts of the Body	109
Illustration 18: An Example of a Mandala	120
Illustration 19: Personal Affirmation	135
Illustration 20: Social Affirmation	138
Illustration 21: A Universal Affirmation	141
Illustration 22: Loving-Kindness Affirmation I	142
Illustration 23: Loving-Kindness Affirmation II	142
Illustration 24: Loving-Kindness Affirmation III	143
Illustration 25: Loving-Kindness Affirmation IV	144
Illustration 26: Pagan Prayer Beads	159
Illustration 27: A Meditation Chant	167
Illustration 28: Walking Meditation Mantra	171
Illustration 29: A Pagan Mandala	176
Illustration 30: A Tarot Labyrinth	180
Illustration 31: A Rune Spiral	183
Illustration 32: The Diagram of Numbers	185
Illustration 33: The Symbolism of Numbers	186
Illustration 34: Number - Letter correspondences	188

Just Being

Appendices

About the Author

Shanddaramon is a published writer, composer, and poet and is the author of several books and articles on living and being a modern Pagan. He lives in the Boston, Massachusetts area with his family where he teaches classes in music. He has often sought ways in which to combine his interest in the arts with a growing interest in the mystical and, specifically, through Paganism. He applies these skills through his art and writing and through services such as divinatory advising, pastoral counseling and ritual work. Combining the arts with mysticism, he has created classes and workshops for others with similar interests and has led rituals for organizations and individuals.

Shanddaramon has led a variety of classes and workshops on meditation throughout his career as an academic and as a community workshop organizer..

Just Being

Appendices

Other Books by Shanddaramon

For Adults:

1. *Self Initiation for the Solitary Witch: Attaining Higher Spirituality Through a Five Degree System.* New Page Books, 2004.
2. *Living Paganism: An Advanced Guide for the Solitary Practitioner.* New Page Books, 2005.
3. *Dewdrops In The Moonlight: A Book of Pagan Prayer.* Astor Press, 2007.
4. *The Sacred Quest: A Pagan Perspective on the Pursuit of Happiness.* Astor Press, 2008.
5. *Paganism: A Religion for the 21st Century.* Astor Press, 2009.

For Children:

1. *Sabbats of the Northern Hemisphere: A Pagan Book for Children.* Astor Press, 2008.
2. *The Twelve Days of Yule: A Pagan Children's Activity Book.* Astor Press, 2009.

Just Being

www.ingramcontent.com/pod-product-compliance
Lightning Source LLC
Chambersburg PA
CBHW032041090426
42744CB00004B/82